Extra Care

Respite, shared
and permanent care
for children with
disabilities

*Hedi Argent and
Ailie Kerrane*

The authors

Hedi Argent is an independent child care and adoption consultant and trainer. She was a guardian *ad litem* for ten years and has had extensive experience of placing children with disabilities. Hedi has written numerous articles for social work journals including *Adoption & Fostering*. She is the author of *Find me a Family*, Souvenir Press, 1983, and the editor of *Keeping the Doors Open*, BAAF, 1988, and *See you Soon: Contact with children who are looked after by local authorities*, BAAF, 1996.

Ailie Kerrane is a social work manager with Bradford Social Services Department. She has worked mainly in adoption and fostering for 25 years. She first became involved in placing children with disabilities for adoption while working with Barnardo's New Families Project in Glasgow in the early 1980s. She is the co-author of *Placing Older and Handicapped Children for Adoption*, Barnardo's, 1985. For the last 18 months, Ailie has been developing fostering services for disabled children and their carers in Bradford.

Contents

(SECTION ONE)

Hedi Argent
What is a disability? Which children need care outside the family? Need and provision. Respite care, foster care, adoption and residential care.

Ailie Kerrane
Background to a new local authority post: Development Officer (Fostering & Disability). The organisation and division of disability services. Systems, policies and specialisation. Diary and comments.

(SECTION TWO)

Hedi Argent
Who's for families? Who chooses to have disabled children? Publicity and recruitment. Projects and campaigns. What do substitute families have a right to expect?

Ailie Kerrane
What carers say about caring. Acting on the results of a survey. Setting up a carers' group. Referrals and recruitment. Proposal for piloting a shared care scheme. Diary and comments.

(SECTION THREE)

Hedi Argent
Working in groups and in families with exercises. Family systems and contact. The significance of gender, ethnicity, culture and religion for disabled children. Attachment and independence. Support networks. Preparing for a real child. Introductions and post-placement services.

Ailie Kerrane
Response to publicity for a shared care pilot project. Information meeting and follow up. Barriers to placement. Preparation/assessment. Diary and comments.

Hedi Argent
Group care as a placement of choice? Assessing residential care. Reviews and liaison. Residential schools and long stay hospitals.

Ailie Kerrane
Residential respite care. No place for permanence. "Warner" interviews for residential work applicants. Information from Perpetrators' Project. The parents' perspective and child protection. Diary and comments.

Hedi Argent
What do children with a disability have a right to expect? Information and explanation. Listening and hearing and keeping the disability factor in mind. Continuity, protection and respect. Preparation to move and planned introductions.

Ailie Kerrane
The child's perspective. Comparing needs. Needs of black disabled children. Planning a move to shared care. Diary and comments.

Hedi Argent
What do parents have a right to expect? Assessments and child care plans. Partnership and support. The tools to make informed decisions. A quality service.

Ailie Kerrane
Learning from parents at home. Visiting parents' support groups. Counselling parents after the birth of a child with Down's Syndrome. Diary and comments.

Hedi Argent
When things don't work out. Disruption and after. Learning how to make it work next time.

Ailie Kerrane
How things work out. What happened to the parents, children and families in the diary.

A note about terminology

Race
The word "race" is placed in inverted commas in the text where colloquially or incorrectly applied to stress that the categorisation of people into different "races" is a social definition – one which has been used to determine hierarchies which have disadvantaged black people. It is not a biological definition as there is only one race, the human race.

Mixed parentage
The term "mixed parentage" has been used in the text to apply to those with one black and one white parent. Wherever possible, this has been further described, as mixed parentage could mean African-Caribbean/white, Asian/white, African-Caribbean/Asian, etc.

Disabled children / children with disabilities
BAAF prefers the use of "children with disabilities" because it more accurately describes the child. Nevertheless both terms are used in this book, as the author explains in the Introduction.

Children with special needs / hard to place children / challenging children
All children have special needs – "hard to place" more aptly describes the placement service than the child. BAAF uses the terms "challenging children" or "children who present a challenge". However, it has been pointed out that the word "challenge" implies a confrontational attitude from the child, whereas it is the carers and workers who perceive themselves as being challenged by the child's disability.

Acknowledgements

We are grateful to the parents, children and carers who have taught us what we know. Their names and their stories have been changed and amalgamated to preserve anonymity, but this book could not have been written without them.

We also thank Phillida Sawbridge and Celia Beckett for their painstaking reading of the manuscript and their helpful comments; Shaila Shah, Head of Communications at BAAF, and Susanne Clarke, her Editorial Assistant, for their constant support and helpfulness; and Bradford Social Services Department for allowing its practice and policies to be scrutinised and discussed. We are further indebted to Philippa Russell for providing such a comprehensive legal framework to set the book in context, and to Lesley Watson at BAAF's Scottish Centre for her note on the Children (Scotland) Act 1995.

MARKS & SPENCER

We are very grateful for the generous financial assistance we have received from Marks & Spencer and the British Toy and Hobby Association towards production costs of this book.

Introduction

Even twenty five years ago, children with disabilities in the UK were rarely placed in foster care and hardly ever considered for adoption. Parents were expected to get on with the job of parenting as best they could or, if they could not, to leave their child in residential care with the minimum of fuss and with the prospect of a lifetime in institutions for their daughter or their son. If infants with only a minor disability were relinquished by their birth mothers, their papers were rubber stamped with "unfit for adoption". My first encounter with this practice in the late 1960s concerned Jamie, a three-month-old boy born with two webbed fingers on each hand. I remember it so clearly not because it shocked me then, but because it shocks me now, to recall how readily I accepted that verdict.

When change came, it came as it often does in social work with a mighty swing of the pendulum. Inspired by pioneering work in the United States,[1] influenced by the seminal British study of *Children who Wait*,[2] and encouraged by experienced adoptive parents, projects were established to find families for children with "special needs". By 1976, too late for Jamie, some of us were seeking and finding families for the most severely and multiply disabled children.

Language also changed, reflecting the shift in social attitudes and the efforts of various pressure groups to raise awareness of disability and the rights of people with disabilities. So "handicapped" children became disabled children and then children with disabilities and finally, children with an impairment. "Mongol" children became Down's Syndrome children and then children with Down's Syndrome. "Mentally handicapped" children became children with learning difficulties and are now children with special educational needs. The subtle differences of meaning are significant because they lead us to focus on the child *as* a child, first and foremost. Language must certainly be used carefully and respectfully, but it should not be used to inhibit expression. In this book the

authors speak both of children with disabilities and of disabled children. The term "disabled" like "handicapped" can be interpreted as a disadvantage imposed by others, but it may be that society's attitudes are inseparable from the issues of impairment.

At the beginning of 1995, Ailie Kerrane was appointed to develop the shared, foster and permanent family services for disabled children in Bradford. She asked me to recommend some recent books to inspire her. She was already familiar with Catherine Macaskill's important study of adoptive families,[3] Philippa Russell's extensive work on respite care[4] and my own book, now twelve years old, which describes the work of one particular agency.[5] There was nothing else; nothing more up to date; nothing like a manual or handbook about placing children with disabilities outside their own families. So we decided to write such a book ourselves.

We then had to agree what to put in and what to leave out. We do not present a comprehensive research and policy review of disabled children who need care away from their families; this has been admirably covered by Philippa Russell in several publications for the Council for Disabled Children (see Appendix D) and by Jenny Morris for the Who Cares? Trust.[6] Both have affected our thinking greatly and we are beholden to them. We also do not offer a guide through the labyrinth of health, education and social services for all children with disabilities, although we refer to those areas in the context of disabled children living away from home. Our aim is modest: to provide a practice guide about assessment of needs, existing choices, and imaginative alternatives for everyone concerned with planning for children with disabilities who have to be separated from their families.

Why and when do children with disabilities need respite, shared, or permanent care? Can residential care ever be the placement of choice for disabled children and should we assess residential homes as thoroughly as substitute families? How should we recruit, prepare and support new families for disabled children? Can we work directly with all children however seriously impaired? How vital then are issues arising from ethnicity, religion and culture for disabled children? How relevant are child protection issues? And how do we work in partnership, not only with caring, striving parents, but also with parents who have neglected or rejected or harmed their disabled children?

These are some of the questions we hope to answer. But like all good answers, they should in turn lead to more questions. Creative child care work must always ask questions and not take "no" for an answer. If I had asked more questions many years ago, Jamie would not have grown up in care.

The material in this guide is organised in six sections followed by several appendices. However, we begin by presenting the legislative framework that must inform social work practice in this area: this has been compiled by Philippa Russell with a contribution from Lesley Watson on the Children (Scotland) Act 1995. The sections of the book then look at identifying the children and assessing needs; finding and recruiting substitute families; training and preparing them; residential care; working with disabled children; and finally, working with parents. By putting work with parents towards the end of the book, rather than, as some may expect, at the beginning, we do not in any way suggest that it

is less important. On the contrary, working with the parents of disabled children is as essential in placement work as in all other services to families who have a child with disabilities. We hope that we have stressed this throughout the book and that this section is a well timed reinforcement of the central team of partnership.

Each of the sections in this guide is divided into two parts. The main text consists of practice guidance and should be read first. The second part is largely made up of a diary and comments which record a practitioner's experience in developing a good local authority service for children with disabilities. We have titled this part "The practice experience" and presented it alongside the main text; in this live record the author explores situations from many angles, and illustrates them with the problems and triumphs encountered on the way, warts and all.

References

1. Sawbridge P, *Opening New Doors*, BAAF, 1975.
2. Rowe J and Lambert L, *Children who Wait*, ABAA, 1973.
3. Macaskill C, *Against the Odds*, BAAF, 1985.
4. Russell P, *Respite Care*, National Children's Bureau, 1992.
5. Argent H, *Find Me a Family*, Souvenir Press, 1984.
6. Morris J, *Gone Missing? A research and policy review of disabled children living away from home*, The Who Cares? Trust, 1995.

PHILIPPA RUSSELL

Some key legislation

The past decade has seen major changes and
developments in children's services, with a range
of new legislation, regulations and guidance.
The major pieces of legislation in England and
Wales which relate to children with learning and
other disabilities are listed below.

I. The Children Act 1989

The Children Act 1989 brought together most
public and private law relating to children and
established a new approach towards services
provided by the local authority social service
departments for children and their families. The
Act provides a legal framework for a new
approach to provision for children with
disabilities, who are now included within the
Act's definition of "children in need" (Section
17). The local authority has particular
responsibility to provide a range of services and
support for children and families. The Children
Act makes specific reference to **children with
disabilities** in four sections, namely:

Section 23(8): the local authority, where
providing accommodation for a child whom they
are looking after and who is disabled, must 'so
far as is reasonably practicable' secure that the
accommodation 'is not unsuitable to his
particular needs'.

Schedule 2, paragraph 2 requires local
authorities to open and maintain a register of
children with disabilities in their area.

Schedule 2, paragraph 3 enables a local
authority to assess a child's needs for the
purpose of the Children Act at the same time as
making assessments under certain other Acts (in
particular the Education Act 1993 and the NHS
and Community Care Act 1970).

Schedule 2, paragraph 9 requires local
authorities to provide services for children with
disabilities which are designed to minimise the
effects of their disabilities and give them the
opportunities to lead lives which are 'as normal
as possible'.

The Children Act 1989 broke new ground in
including disabled children within a common
regulatory framework for *all* children and the
specific requirements relating to disability must
therefore be met in the context of the 'five
great principles' of the Act, namely:

- *The paramount welfare of the child* (which
  must over-ride parental preferences or any
  other issues);

- *Partnership with parents* (local authorities
  have a duty to try and support parents
  without the use of compulsory powers.
  Parents in turn have 'enduring parental
  responsibility' for their children, whether or
  not the child is living with them);

- *The importance of families* (ie. children
  should be brought up within their own
  immediate or extended families if at all
  possible);

- *The importance of the views of children and
  parents* (local authorities have a duty to
  ascertain and take account of the wishes and
  feelings of parents and children);

- *Corporate responsibility* (the Children Act
  addresses the local authority as a whole, not
  just social services departments. Child health
  services also have duties to co-operate with
  social services departments in fulfilling their
  duties under the Act).

The inclusion of disabled children within the
child protection procedures of the Children Act
has been challenging for everyone, but there is
growing awareness not only of the vulnerability
of disabled children to all forms of abuse, but of
the importance of *listening* to disabled children
about their lives and experiences.

Many disabled children spend periods of time
away from home, whether within respite or
short-term care provisions, or in residential
education or group care. The revision of the
Looked After Children materials[1] now includes

3

material specific to disability, but within the framework of assessment for *all* children and young people.

Volume 6 of the Children Act Guidance and Regulations, *Children with Disabilities,*[2] provides detailed guidance on the provisions of the Children Act 1989 with specific reference to disabled children and their families and on arrangements when disabled children are living or staying away from home. Readers may also find it useful to read the Social Services Inspectorate *Report of the National Inspection of Services for Children with Disabilities*[3] which sets out the standards which the SSI would expect to find in a local authority when offering services to disabled children and their families.

2. The Chronically Sick and Disabled Persons Act 1970

This Act places various duties upon local authorities with reference to disabled people of all ages, including disabled children as defined in Section 17 of the Children Act 1989.

Section 1: In particular the Act requires local authorities (Section 1) to identify the numbers of disabled people in their area and to publish information about social services provided under Section 2 of the Act in their area.

Section 2: This section requires local authorities to make arrangements for a number of social services if they are satisfied that it is necessary for them to do so to meet a disabled person's needs. These services include practical assistance in the home; facilities for or assistance with travelling to and from home; adaptations to the home; holidays and provision or assistance in obtaining a telephone.

The Act is summarised in Annex B of the DoH guidance on *Children with Disabilities*.[4]

3. The Disabled Persons (Services, Consultation and Representation) Act 1986

This Act supplements the provisions of the Chronically Sick and Disabled Persons Act 1970 and applies to disabled children and adults.

Section 4 requires local authorities to assess needs for services under Section 2 of the 1970 Act.

Sections 5 and 6 require local authorities to identify disabled school leavers and assess their needs for social services. This duty is significant with reference to the new requirement for LEAs to make Transition Plans for young people with special educational needs and statements at the 14 plus Annual Review (see section on Education Act 1993).

The Disabled Persons Act is further summarised in Annex B of the DoH guidance on *Children with Disabilities.*[5]

4. Local Government and Housing Act 1989

Section 114 of the Local Government and Housing Act enables local authorities to give disabled facilities grants to disabled people (including children) to help with the costs of adaptations to enable them to live as independently as possible in their own homes.

5. The National Health Service and Community Care Act 1990

The NHS and Community Care Act 1990 provides the legal framework for the provision of health care for children and adults in England and Wales. Readers may find it helpful to refer to the Department of Health's guidance on *The Welfare of Children and Young People in Hospital*[6] and their parallel guidance on *Child Health in the Community: A guide to good practice.*[7] Section 27 of the Children Act 1989 provides for co-operation between housing authorities, social services departments, education authorities and health authorities and NHS Trusts.

The same Act provides the legal framework for the provision of community care. Purchasers and providers of children's services will wish to liaise with those working in adult services to ensure that children's services are acknowledged within local community care planning arrangements. A full list of the extensive community care guidance can be obtained from the Department of Health's Publications Unit (address at the end of this chapter).

As the pattern of childhood disability changes, with increasing numbers of very severely disabled children surviving through improvements in neonatal and other medical care, the Community Care debate about what constitutes continuing health care needs is growing in momentum. Originally a debate which focused primarily upon the care of the elderly (and the shift from health to local authority or private residential care), the issue is now live for children who may require very complex support services from the NHS in order to live in their local communities. Readers should therefore ensure that they are aware of both national guidance and local guidelines with reference to disabled children and other users of community care.

6. The Carers (Recognition and Services) Act 1995

The Carers (Recognition and Services) Act was implemented in 1996. The Act provides for carers to request and to receive independent assessments of their needs when the person cared for is undergoing an assessment under Section 47 of the National Health Services and Community Care Act 1990 or the Children Act 1989 or the Chronically Sick and Disabled Persons Act. The results of the carer's assessment should be taken into account when the local authority is making decisions about services to be provided to the user. Carers are defined as those who are either providing or intend to provide regular

and substantial care. The definition includes young carers. *The Carers (Recognition and Services) Act 1995: Policy Guidance and Practice Guide*[8] is available from the Department of Health's Publications Unit (address at the end of this chapter).

7. Community Care (Direct Payments) Act 1996

The Community Care (Direct Payments) Act 1996 is designed to enable local authorities to make direct payments to service users so that they can purchase their own community care. Currently, Regulations under the Act only apply to physically disabled adults but will be extended. There has been widespread support for the Bill, but there were some initial concerns when disabled people did not realise that they might become employers in their own right and have to take account of existing regulations on payment of national insurance and taxation for staff. Under the Independent Living Fund, some disabled people have received very large retrospective tax and NI bills for their care staff because they had not been given advice on how to become a good employer. When the Act extends to younger age groups, parents should therefore take advice from organisations like the Disability Alliance, which have printed advice available (see Appendix E).

The extent to which parents or foster carers would wish to become "purchasers" for their children's community support services is not yet clear. Many parents would prefer to have a service brokerage model of support, with the social services department acting as "broker" for an appropriate mix of local services. But other parents have argued that, with relatively modest resources, they could purchase their own support and this might include reimbursing relatives or friends for providing any additional care. Whether or not the Act is extended to cover children, it raises important issues about how packages of care are put together for parents and children and whether some parents might not make very effective managers for their children's services.

8. Short Term Breaks (Disabled Persons and Carers) Bill 1996

In 1995, the Department of Health amended the regulations relating to the provision of respite care under the Children Act 1989, extending the number of days from 90 to 120 and introducing greater flexibility with regard to medical examinations and visits to the placement. The changes reflected recognition that whilst quality could only be ensured by rigorous recruitment, assessment and planning, the previous regulations (which related to foster placements) were more appropriate for children living than staying away from home. As many disabled children use respite care on an occasional basis (some not even staying overnight), the procedures were found to be burdensome, expensive and inappropriate. The new flexibility has been generally welcomed by parents and social services departments alike.

However, the relaxation of regulations relating to respite care and the regulatory framework of the Children Act 1989 did not clarify the right of carers to have access to good quality respite or short-term care or address the absence of specific requirements to provide respite or short-term care within the Children Act, NHS and Community Care Act or the Carers (Recognition and Services) Act 1995. The Short Term Breaks (Disabled Persons and Carers) Bill was therefore introduced to address respite or short-term care across all disabilities and age groups and was received very favourably within the House of Lords. Although the Bill in its present form is most unlikely to get through Parliament prior to the General Election, the Bill is worth noting for its widespread support for clarifying the rights of families to respite or short-term care – and the recognition that for many families (whether birth or substitute) good quality respite care will be a critical component in any package to enable them to continue to care for their disabled children at home.

9. The Disability Discrimination Act 1995

Following a consultation on disability and discrimination, the Government introduced a Bill in 1995 to ensure that disabled people have equal opportunities in terms of access to employment, buildings, services and the environment in general. The Act was implemented in 1996 and will be monitored by an independent National Disability Council. Although much of the legislation relates primarily to adults, Section 29 of the Act requires schools to report annually on their admission procedures for disabled children; on arrangements for access (which includes access to the curriculum as well as physical access), and the measures the school proposes to take to prevent any discrimination against disabled pupils. Section 20 of the Act requires colleges of further education and institutions in the higher education sector to produce disability statements on their access and admission arrangements and on any special facilities which may be offered to disabled students.

The Act also addresses discrimination in a variety of settings, including the health service; social services (day care, holiday schemes and respite care are covered); housing, leisure and employment, as well as the use of services such as shops, hotels, sports provision, etc. A Code of Practice on Access to Services will be made available.

10. The Education Acts 1993 and 1996

In 1996, the Government decided to consolidate a number of different pieces of recent education legislation within a single consolidated Act, the Education Act 1996. The 1993 Education Act is therefore now subsumed within the 1996 Act.

The Education Act 1996 provides the legal framework for assessment and making special educational provision for children with special education needs, and is accompanied by the Department of Education's *Code of Practice on the Identification and Assessment of Special Educational Needs*,[9] which provides comprehensive guidance on the five stages of assessment, starting with school-based procedures and moving on to statutory assessment and review.

The Code of Practice emphasises the importance of partnership with parents and with pupils and introduces the role of the 'named person' or parent adviser and befriender. Parents have the new right of independent appeal to the Special Educational Needs Tribunal.

The Code of Practice introduces the new 14-plus Transition Plan, which replaces the former 13-plus statutory re-assessment. This requires the local education authority (LEA) to consult with social services departments, the health authority, the careers service and the Further Education Funding Council in planning for the young person's transition to adult life.

11. The Nursery Education and Grant Maintained Schools Act 1995

This Act introduces the Government's controversial nursery voucher scheme. The Special Educational Consortium (which is established under the auspices of the Council for Disabled Children) has strenuously opposed the voucher system on the grounds that it requires expensive administration; it cannot offer choice when there is insufficient educational nursery provision and it offers a 'fixed tariff' voucher (with the risk that disabled children may not be offered places because they are seen as too expensive). There is particular concern about how the voucher redeeming services will firstly be approved and registered and secondly how they will be inspected. The Office for Standards in Education (OFSTED) will carry out the inspections, but there are concerns about the numbers of inspectors available to do the work.

For the time being (given the insufficiency of nursery education places), playgroups, social services day nurseries and nurseries run by independent or voluntary agencies may apply for voucher status. It is not yet clear what qualified education staff will have to be available within establishments which are not educational in origin. The nursery voucher scheme currently only applies to four-year-olds, but the Government hopes to lower the age to three in due course. The vouchers can be used to pay for Portage and similar home teaching programmes for children with special educational needs, if the parents wish it.

12. The Mental Health Act 1983

The Mental Health Act 1983 is largely concerned with adults. Children and young people with mental health difficulties will usually be provided for under children's legislation such as the Children Act 1989 and the NHS and Community Care Act 1990. However, the Mental Health Act 1983 is important because it clearly separates definitions of learning disability from mental illness. It gives young people of 16 and over the right to give consent to treatment except in an emergency and it provides arrangements for guardianship of young people of 16 and over. Guardianship in this context is a limited activity designed to protect a vulnerable person or to ensure that they receive treatment. A free *Highlight* on the Mental Health Act is available from the Council for Disabled Children.[10]

13. Children's Services Planning Order (SI 1996, No. 785)

In 1996, the Government introduced mandatory Children's Services Plans. This amendment to the Children Act 1989 requires local authorities to:

- assess the need for provision in their area for services provided under Part III of the Children Act 1989 (ie. for children regarded as being "in need");

- to consult with various bodies as to how these needs should be met;

- to publish and regularly review the resulting plans.

Children's Services Plans will be very important opportunities for parents of disabled children to make certain that their views are represented and to influence the way in which services are developed. Although social services departments take the lead, the plans are interagency and social services must consult with:

● health authorities and NHS trusts

● LEAs and grant maintained schools

● voluntary and consumer organisations

● the police and probation services.

The Children's Services Plan must include services for children with disabilities and their families and all local authorities will be expected to implement the existing requirement to have a Register of Children with Disabilities in their areas. The emphasis in the guidance is on the "whole child" and the guidance for LEAs (from the Department for Education and Employment (DFEE)) states that:

> 'it [the plan] should also address how the needs of disabled children can be met by services in non-segregated settings wherever possible.'

Plans are expected to show clear, targeted and timed objectives which will be regularly reviewed.

Further information is available in *Children's Services Planning: Guidance* available from the Department of Health Publications Unit (address below).

The Citizen's Charter

It is important to remember that all public services should pay attention to the key messages in the Citizen's Charter, namely, that people are entitled to access to full and accurate information about services and performance; "informed choice", "value for money" and an effective complaints procedure. *The Patient's Charter: Services for Children and Young People* is available free from the NHS Executive (0800 555777).[12]

Monitoring the legislation

In the UK, legislation provides only the "framework"; understanding the regulations and guidance is essential and to do this, it is useful to read reports and review documents from government departments.

OFSTED provides the inspection arrangements for schools and publishes regular free reports on each school visited. It also provides a wider range of reports (a new report on the implementation of the Code of Practice will be published by early 1997). Some of these reports may be charged for. For further details, write to OFSTED, Alexandra House, Kingsway, London WC2B 6SE.

The Social Services Inspectorate (SSI) inspects social services in England and Wales. It also publishes regular reports on inspection visits. A full list is available from the Department of Health's Wetherby Publications Unit (address on following page). The SSI also publishes national reports, for example, the report of the first inspection of services for disabled children under the Children Act 1989. Some reports are free; others will be charged for.

The NHS Executive publishes a range of reports on health services in England and Wales. You should be able to see the full range of these reports at your local Community Health Council's office.

Audit Commission reports provide useful national overviews of how different services are developing and where the problem areas are. These reports are published by the Audit Commission and HMSO and have to be purchased. You can borrow them through your local library which should have full lists of what is available. The Audit Commission reports regularly on issues relating to education, health and social services and community care.

Getting more information

A full list of the extensive community care guidance can be obtained from the Department of Health's Publications Unit, Wetherby Stores, PO Box 40, Wetherby LS29 7NL. Their publication lists indicate those items which are available free on request and those which may be purchased from HMSO (Her Majesty's Stationery Office).

Copies of all legislation and regulations relating to services in the United Kingdom can be purchased from the HMSO (Her Majesty's Stationery Office). A telephone ordering system operates on 0l7l 873 9090.

Copies of the *Code of Practice on the Identification and Assessment of Special Educational Needs* are available free from the Department for Education and Employment, Sanctuary Buildings, Great Smith Street, London SW l. *The Parents' Guide to the Code of Practice* is also free from the same address and offers a useful short guide for professionals as well as parents who wish to 'get in on the Act'.

Information material on the Disability Discrimination Act l995 is available free through a direct telephone ordering system (0345 622 633). *The Disability Discrimination Act l995: A guide for everybody*[13] is a useful introduction to the Act and is available free from this number. Copies of publications relating to the Act which must be purchased (in particular the *Code of Practice on Rights of Access – Goods, Facilities, Services and Premises*) are available through HMSO (telephone number above).

Philippa Russell is the Director of the Council for Disabled Children at the National Children's Bureau.

References

1. Department of Health, *Looking after Children: Good Parenting, good outcomes*, HMSO, 1995.
2. Department of Health, The Children Act Guidance and Regulations, Vol 6, *Children with Disabilities*, HMSO, 1991.
3. Department of Health, Social Services Inspectorate, *Report of the National Inspection of Services for Children with Disabilities*, HMSO, 1994.
4. See 2 above.
5. See 2 above.
6. Department of Health, *The Welfare of Children and Young People in Hospital*, HMSO, 1991.
7. Department of Health, *Child Health in the Community: A guide to good practice*, HMSO, 1996.
8. Department of Health, *The Carers (Recognition and Services) Act 1995: Policy guidance and practice guide* (two volumes), Department of Health, 1996.
9. Department of Education, *Code of Practice on the Identification and Assessment of Special Educational Needs*, Department of Education, 1994.
10. Russell P, *Highlight no. 73, The Mental Health Act – A Summary*, National Children's Bureau, 1986.
11. Department of Health, *Children's Services Planning: Guidance*, LAC (96) 10, Department of Health/Department of Education and Employment, 1996.
12. Department of Health, *The Patient's Charter: Services to Children and Young People*, 1996.
13. *The Disability Discrimination Act 1995: A guide for everybody*, DL60, DSS, October 1996.

LESLEY WATSON

The **Children (Scotland) Act** 1995

Whilst much of the legislation about community care and disability in England and Wales also applies to Scotland, the Children (Scotland) Act 1995 provides the cornerstone for policy, planning and service provision to children with disabilities.[1] There are a number of important provisions in this Act which will require local authorities to re-evaluate what they currently offer to children with disabilities and their families and should ultimately result in more accessible and better co-ordinated services.

Children in Need

This concept specifically includes children with disabilities as in the Children Act 1989, but it also recognises children who are affected adversely by the disability of any other person in their family, as "children in need". Thus, not only should the needs of child carers be addressed, but there is a recognition that, for example, having a sibling who is disabled in some way has implications for all the other children within the family.

The legislation requires each local authority to provide a range and level of services which safeguard and promote the welfare of children within its area who are "in need" and which promote the upbringing of such children within their family (Section 22). Section 23(2) states that a person is said to be disabled if he or she is chronically sick or disabled, or suffers from a disorder within the meaning of the Mental Health (Scotland) Act 1984. The local authority is specifically required by Section 23(1), when providing services to children in need, to design these services in such a way as to minimise the effect of an impairment or to minimise the effect of a child's disability on any other person in his or her family. The stated aim is that all children should have the opportunity to lead lives which are as normal as possible and it thus offers local authorities the opportunity to develop and promote services which can support disabled children within their family and their local community. The Act also states that in providing these services the local authority shall 'have regard so far as practicable' to each child's religion, and racial, cultural and linguistic origins.

Planning

Section 19 of the Children (Scotland) Act requires local authorities to prepare and publish plans for the provision of the "relevant services" for children in their area, and these include services for children with disabilities. The Act promotes co-operation between a variety of agencies including Health Boards, National Health Service Trusts, the Reporter to the Children's Panel and the local Children's Panel Chairperson. The responsibility for preparing these plans lies with the Chief Executive; thus local authorities are expected to undertake a comprehensive, objective evaluation of current service provision and to identify how they will assess and provide for unmet need in their area. The Act also specifies that relevant voluntary organisations have to be consulted during the process of preparing the Children's Services Plans, thus recognising that they already play a valuable role in providing well-established services to some children with disabilities.

Throughout the Act there is an emphasis on the notion of partnership between the local authority and the parent and the child. The process of producing these plans offers an ideal opportunity to put this theme into practice by involving parents and children/young people at each stage in the process.

Assessment

Section 23 of the Children (Scotland) Act states that the local authority must assess the needs of a child who is disabled or affected by disability when requested to do so by a child's parent or guardian, and thus that in carrying out their obligation to provide services which will safeguard and promote the welfare of children in their area, they are taking account of and providing for children with disabilities. Under Section 24 the carer may also request that the local authority undertake an assessment of their ability to provide care for that child as long as they are providing a 'substantial amount' of care on a regular basis and are not doing so as a volunteer or as a worker.

Service delivery

Section 27 of the Act requires that each local authority provide such day care as is appropriate for children in need who are aged five years or under and have not started school. They are also required to provide such care as is appropriate to children in need who are of school age outside school hours and during school holidays. Again this will include children with disabilities or affected by disability. A large number of families who have children with disabilities have made use of the gradually increasing provisions for respite care which exist throughout Scotland – both residential and family based respite. Where a placement is made in accommodation provided by the local authority which lasts for more than 24 hours, the child becomes a "looked after" child under Section 25. This means that such placements will have more formality than was previously the case, and although the Scottish Office Guidance has taken account of the special nature of these placements, the child will still be expected to have a medical prior to the first placement, for example, and will be subject to statutory reviews. Carers may well find themselves subject to more rigorous assessment similar to that required for fostering. Many parents have accepted the provision of respite for their child on the basis that they would not be "in care"

and this change in status is bound to cause some concern even if it has been done in order to provide them with additional safeguards about the placement their child will be going to. It also will mean that the local authority will have additional duties to these children under Section 17 including that of safeguarding and promoting his/her welfare. They will also have responsibilities under Section 29 relating to after–care if the young person is still receiving respite when they 'cease to be of school age'.

Section 17 also requires the local authority 'so far as is reasonably practicable' to ascertain the views of the child, his/her parents and anyone who has parental rights in relation to him/her before making any decisions with respect to a child whom they are looking after. This underpins a principle which runs throughout the Act that the views of children and young people should be sought and taken into account in all matters relating to them.

Conclusion

The provision of services to children with or affected by disability is an area which has seen some improvement over recent years as a result of the community care legislation and practice. The Children (Scotland) Act will allow local authorities to build on what is already there so that the needs of disabled children, young people and their families can be met in ways which are more responsive to individuals and are better co-ordinated than previously.

Lesley Watson is a Trainer/Consultant at BAAF, Scotland

Reference

1.   *The Children (Scotland) Act 1995: Training programme*, BAAF, 1996.

Identifying the children and assessing needs

What is a disability?

The UK government's definition of disability is taken from the Disability Discrimination Act 1995:

A physical or mental impairment which has substantial and long-term effect on the ability to carry out normal day-to-day activities.

There is also a "social model" definition which defines disability in terms of the combined effects of impairment and social oppression. It takes into account the role that society plays in disabling a person with impairments, thereby preventing their full participation in society due to cultural, physical and social barriers which take little account of people with an impairment.

For the purposes of this book we consider case examples that look at the extra care that children with disabilities will need based on 'a restriction or lack of ability to perform an activity in the manner or within the range considered to be normal ...' (World Health Organisation). However, it is implicit throughout the book that these children will encounter societal barriers at different stages in their lives and that these will also influence the care plan.

Which children need care outside the family?

The majority of children with disabilities who come to the attention of social services continue to live in their own homes for most of the time. They are nevertheless children "in need", according to the 1989 Children Act, and qualify for a whole range of specialist services.

The birth of a disabled child is a traumatic experience for most families; shock, grief and anger have to be followed by constant adjustments and readjustments. The anxiety and tiredness associated with having children can become overwhelming when the child is disabled. And the tiredness and anxiety may increase as the child gets older and heavier, whereas parents can rightly expect the pressures to ease as their other children grow up. Painful decisions have to be made, marriages are put under strain and other children in the family may suffer. Added to this, it is said to cost three times more to bring up a disabled child than one who is not.[1] No wonder that families look for relief.

A national survey of over a thousand parents has explored the needs and circumstances of families caring for a severely disabled child.[2] The research sought parents' views of their child's needs as well as their experiences as service users. Comparisons with data collected twenty years ago indicate little improvement in the circumstances in which families are caring for their severely disabled child. The researchers found the following:

- Severely disabled children of all ages are highly dependent on their parents to meet their basic care and treatment needs. In addition, older children are likely to have social, communication and behavioural problems.

- One in two of the children under two years was dependent on at least one item of medical equipment.

- On average, household incomes were lower among these families compared with families with non-disabled children. Nine out of ten lone parents, and over a third of two parent families, had no income other than benefits.

- Over four out of ten families said their housing was unsuitable for caring for a disabled child; difficult stairs, lack of space, and cold and damp were common problems.

- Only half the sample described their relationship with professionals as positive and supportive.

- The most common unmet needs of the child related to learning skills, meeting physical needs, and having someone to discuss their disability with.

- The most common unmet needs of the parents were financial resources, help in planning the child's future, help with care, and knowledge of available services.

- Certain groups were particularly vulnerable to high levels of unmet need and poor living circumstances. They included families from minority ethnic groups, lone parent families and those caring for the most severely impaired children.

Potentially, all parents with a disabled child are under stress and at risk of having a crisis at some time which they will not be able to handle on their own. They may ask for financial help, for respite care, for boarding schools, for domiciliary services, for some form of shared care or they may even enquire about residential care or adoption.

For disabled children, as for all children, it is imperative to explore the possibility of supporting placements with relatives in the first instance. Whatever parents ask for, their desire for relief is not the same as rejection. Not being able to look after their own child, full time or even part time, does not usually mean that they want to disengage completely.

Emily was born with Down's Syndrome one year after her sister Zoe. She also had a severe heart defect which would require surgery before she was five, but the prognosis for her survival until then was poor. Her young parents were totally unprepared for looking after a child with disabilities.

B RADFORD *delivers its services to children with disabilities through two separate divisions of the Directorate: a Children's Division and a Disability and Community Health Division. As a result disabled children receive different services from both. The structure does not lend itself to creating a coherent and overall set of policies regarding service provision for children with disabilities. All provision specifically for disabled children lies within the Disability Division ie. respite care (both residential and family based), specialist workers and outreach support. However, there are a significant number of disabled children within the looked after system, and the services to them and their families – social work, fostering and adoption – are provided through the Children's Division.*

The Adoption and Fostering Unit – part of the Children's Division – is a large, centralised service working with approximately 400 carers of all kinds, from adoption through to time-limited, task-centred fostering. All foster carers are fee paid. The work is carried out within three teams – one focusing on the needs of children up to eight years old, one on children/young people over nine years; and one, the Initial Response Team, providing the front line service to mainstream workers who request immediate placements. This team also deals with recruitment and information for the public, and manages the post-adoption service. Disabled children are placed within this mainstream service – but no separate specialist provision is made.

The Children's and Disability Divisions have separate structures and staffing, and although attempts have been made to forge links and keep communication open, there are inevitably yawning gaps. The recognition of these gaps led to the establishment of a small but important project with three seconded workers (representing both divisions) examining over a three-month period the fostering needs of disabled children within the looked after system. The project produced an excellent report, completed in December 1993, which clearly identified problems and made a series of recommendations to improve communication between the Divisions and enhance service delivery. My current post of Development Officer (Fostering and Disability) was created to implement these recommendations and continue the process of identifying blocks and barriers to providing good services for disabled children.

In my contribution to this book I will attempt to bring alive the day-to-day dilemmas of tackling these issues and of trying to see "the wood for the trees".

They knew nothing about Down's Syndrome and were too embarrassed to tell their friends and colleagues about Emily. They were afraid that their marriage and their whole lifestyle would collapse and they felt that they had a duty to protect their first child, Zoe.

At their request, Emily was placed with foster carers who had extensive experience of disability, when she was four weeks old and allowed to leave hospital. The parents visited daily. They introduced Zoe to her new sister. They learned from the foster carers how to look after Emily. They were given time and counselling to make informed choices. They could consult with the paediatrician and heart specialist without being worn out. After two months they decided to take Emily home, but they soon found that they couldn't manage both children on a day–to–day basis. Emily went back to the same foster carers and the parents had her every week end. She became established as a member of her family although she lived with another family for the greater part of each week.

This was an open, shared care arrangement, supported by an enlightened disability team in a local authority. As time went on, Emily came home for longer periods and when she had her operation at the age of four, the parents took complete charge. Emily survived the surgery and now lives with her own family; her foster carers offer regular respite which the parents gratefully accept. If they ask for more at any time in the future, they know that it will be available. The social services team continues to monitor progress and need.

An accepting approach from service providers will not always help to keep the child in the family. For Susan, it was the other way round.

Susan was a child with multiple physical and learning disabilities due to Angelman Syndrome. Her parents managed well enough, refusing all offers of help from social services, until they had a second child when Susan was four. Then they asked for respite care for Susan one weekend a month. Susan was made

welcome in a local home for children with disabilities which held a small number of beds for respite care. Susan liked going to the home and she and her family were befriended by a female member of staff. After a while the parents asked for every other weekend and after a year, Susan was spending every Friday to Monday in the children's home. By this time, Susan seemed as attached to her key worker as to her mother.

Everyone agreed that family life was better for Susan than spending half her time in a home, and the key worker, who was leaving to get married, was approved to become Susan's foster carer. Susan spent less and less time at home, but the parents now visited her regularly in the foster home. After another two years, the foster carers applied to adopt Susan with the full support of the parents and the local authority. Susan was duly adopted and her parents then became the respite carers, having Susan to stay with them one weekend a month.

What the above cases demonstrate is the need for flexible services for children with disabilities. Both sets of parents were well intentioned people, struggling to find the best way for their child and for themselves. Both local authorities offered a continuum of provision, ranging from respite care, through shared and foster care, to adoption. The families did not have to disentangle the procedures and policies of different departments and they were never made to feel that they were making unreasonable demands or that they were failing as parents.

If Emily and Susan had been less well served by their local authorities, either or both could have ended up in long-term care; Emily's parents might have been forced to come to a clear cut decision before they were ready, and for purely bureaucratic reasons; they could have taken Emily home without mutual agreement, persevered until the first crisis and then given up in despair and with resentment towards all social workers. Such stress could exacerbate marital discord and lead to family break-up.

Even in a development post which is specifically created to look at services from a more objective standpoint, it is easy to become enmeshed in the complex strands of individual views, lack of resources, and the many other dynamics which affect disabled children and young people whose lives are caught up in this web.

I have kept a diary, separate from the official Departmental record, in order to reflect on the emerging issues and my learning. This diary forms the basis of most of my material here.

15 March 95

Coming to this post, with the remit of ensuring better quality of care for disabled children in the looked after system, I am immediately presented with a serious challenge at the first step:
– Who are the children?
– What does "disabled" mean?
One of the most difficult areas will be to find the disabled children in the "looked after" population. We seem to be working in the dark. An information system adequate to our needs is unlikely to be in place for perhaps up to two years from now.

17 March 95

So far, the method used to identify the children has been to ask all the social workers in the Adoption and Fostering Unit to list the disabled children they know of. This has in turn led to an interesting debate around terminology and definitions. Within the unit, the various terms – disabled, special needs, learning difficulty – tend to be used interchangeably and indiscriminately, whereas colleagues within the Disability Division are much more specific. This affects service delivery. For example, to qualify for respite care, a child must have a recognised serious disability and the family must be under severe stress with a risk of family breakdown. In the mainstream child care services, the criteria used are either child protection or the need for accommodation; defining the child's disability is therefore of secondary importance in this context.

These differences of emphasis make identification of a particular population of children problematic. Even when we have suitable systems in place, we won't know for whom we are providing until we have agreed a definition of disability. So far I have simply worked with and accepted the differences in approach and allowed a wide variation in definition. This has not yet presented a problem, but I can see it will once we move further into looking at service provision and, for example, the development of a shared care scheme.

The original report identified 35 disabled children currently living with foster carers and therefore primarily receiving services through the Children's Division. Although the definition of disability used was very broad, the authors indicated that almost half of those on the list could be clearly viewed as having profound difficulties, including several "special care" young people. The majority of children on the list will require long-term support services geared to their individual needs. However, the list was compiled more than 18 months ago, and I have no way of knowing which other children might subsequently have joined this group, and so should also be a target for any new services or information. The problem of devising and constantly updating a system to identify disabled children within the looked after category is a continuing one for which, as yet, there seems to be no solution.

21 March 95

Decided to try to compile a register of carers interested in caring for disabled children. Started with the 35 households on the Project list, but that now needs updating. It was only a snapshot. Some of those children will have moved on – how do I find out this information? Memo to all Unit workers?

28 March 95

Must identify specific children needing a fostering resource and have contacted Children's Disabilities Team in the Disability Division to get this going.

The scene could have been set for a series of foster homes for Emily, decreasing family contact and drift. Susan could have remained in long term residential care if the local authority had not moved as easily between one form of care and another. She would then have lost not only her parents but also her key worker. And her parents would have been less likely to agree to family placement if it were later suggested, because they would not have believed that another family could do what they themselves could not. The local authority might, in the end, have applied for care orders in both cases, to enable long-term plans to be made. Everything would then militate against working in partnership with the parents.

Unfortunately, many children with disabilities come into the care system along similar routes to the ones Emily and Susan might have travelled. Others are accommodated by local authorities because they need specialist or total care which their parents cannot provide, or perhaps, cannot go on and on providing. Some are under court orders because they have been neglected or abused as some non-disabled children are. Relatively few are abandoned just because they are disabled.

A large group of disabled children have been placed almost permanently in boarding schools by their parents and a few live in hospitals; they are not the responsibility of the local authority unless they are being "looked after", but local authorities have a duty to take reasonable steps to ensure that their welfare is being adequately safeguarded and promoted. However, there is an increasing tendency for local authorities which have closed down their own residential units, to use specialist boarding schools for 52 weeks a year, when family placements fail or have not been found. Residential schools are not an alternative to residential care. They should only be considered if the child requires education not available in day schools. Even then, the need for very special education has to be weighed against the need for appropriate care; at least a permanent holiday family should be found. All children who are separated from their families have special needs and deserve our very best

service. Children with disabilities have extra needs and we may have to make the impossible happen for them.

Need and provision

Respite care

The words "respite care" imply only relief for parents, but respite care should and can also be a positive experience for the child. Need is here easily confused with available provision. For instance, respite care may be offered to fit in with administrative convenience rather than with a family's lifestyle.

> *Helen, a single adoptive parent, lived in an area where she was entitled to twenty one days of respite care a year for her son David, who had spina bifida. Helen wanted to be able to have breaks as and when she and David most needed them, but she was faced with having to book each January for the whole year ahead.*

> *The Lane family had three children with disabilities and their local authority was most generous with respite care. Although the family planned ahead, the respite care was never available for all three children at the same time. The parents would gladly have accepted less, if they could have only had one week a year to themselves.*

There are many respite care schemes which give a service when and how families want it, both in residential homes and family settings. It is possible to find ways to satisfy parents who want to plan well ahead and also to respond to those who want respite whenever they most need it. Some authorities link parents directly with respite carers and some give vouchers which can be used as required.

Most social services departments recognise that disabled foster and adopted children also have a right to respite care. There may be instances where respite care may not be accessible to all who need it.

11 April 95 Have to chase up that list of possible children needing placement. I know the problem is lack of staff resources – quite a few workers off sick at the moment, therefore no time for developmental tasks like this.

1 May 95 Meeting with Senior Care Manager in the Adoption and Fostering Unit. Discussed the following issues:

A system is required to identify disabled children currently fostered or waiting for placement. It's a bit haphazard whether, on the current lists of children referred to the Unit for long–term placement, there is any indication if they are disabled or not. It may be noted on the referral form, and certainly individual workers probably know, but this is not always transferred to the main list, so summarising or monitoring disability needs is impossible.

It would also be useful to have a system of identifying and monitoring potential applicants interested in caring for a child with disabilities. Again, this would be noted on their individual file, but not necessarily anywhere else (until they are approved, of course).

These would be useful tasks for me to undertake, ie. monitoring referrals of both children and potential placements. But we need a system in place in order to do this.

It is clear that the lack of good, clear monitoring and recording remains a major problem. I still feel rather defeated by this one. I'm not skilled or qualified in designing systems, and the feedback I get from those who are is that there is nothing that can be done in the short term although the long–term goal is a comprehensive computerised system for the whole department. Meanwhile, I'll have to find some way of gathering information more coherently.

I have already observed that the structure of the Department does not lend itself to a unified plan for service provision for disabled children who are looked after.

My post, which focuses on the foster care needs of disabled children, is proving effective within that remit, but while I can identify problems created by the various strategies and policies pursued over the last few years, I am not in a position within the structure of the department, to enable issues to be tackled strategically.

5 May 95 An interesting point I may not have noted before is that the lack of any residential provision, other than respite, is deliberate. It was a view held very strongly by a senior manager that provision of full-time residential care for children with disabilities was bad because it encouraged drift and lack of planning with the danger of children being "forgotten". As a result, disabled children in Bradford have been cared for full–time in respite units. This manager has now retired and it is acknowledged that some children may need residential care, but it is still only provided within respite settings.

This doesn't make sense to me. Either we accept that some children will require a spell in residential care and provide an appropriate setting or we do not. It is probably quite an important issue for me given that the Adoption and Fostering Unit may be asked to find family placements for these children.

In raising the issue of residential care with managers within both the Children's and Disability Divisions, it became clear to me that while it was recognised as a problem, there was no obvious or logical place within the structure to develop, debate, and take forward a strategy regarding residential provision which would clearly have both policy and resource implications.

A case example underlines how this structural problem affects individual children in a profound way.

Some minority ethnic groups have limited knowledge of the role of the local authority and therefore their rights to services such as respite care. Or they may be too protective of their disabled children to ask for outside help. There could be problems of communication as well as isolation. Unless there is a policy of outreach work and positive targeting, families could experience double discrimination.

A few hospitals still offer respite places, but should only be used as part of an overall plan linked to special needs.[3]

Whatever the programme, whether it involves residential care or respite carers, it will only fulfil a need if it is based on a careful assessment and tailored to fit the family, not the system.

Respite care ought to be a satisfying event for the whole family if the child enjoys it and the parents know it is enjoyable.

Foster care

Short-term foster care for children with disabilities serves the same purpose as for any other children: as a response to an emergency, as a refuge in times of crisis, or as a bridge between more permanent arrangements. It is essential that foster carers should know what is expected of them, that their rights and interests are protected, and that their agreement to limit themselves to a short-term service is respected. At the same time, there must be some flexibility if short-term foster care is part of a comprehensive service for disabled children, who should only leave a placement to go back to their own homes or to move to a permanent substitute home.

It is more important to inform foster carers about the needs and circumstances of each child than to maintain a strict time schedule. Emily might never have returned to her parents if her short-term foster carer had not been able to wait for them to make their decisions. A series of moves could have damaged Emily's ability to attach, and consequently, her parents' growing confidence in handling her.

Long-term foster care, now unloved by many local authorities, still has a part to play. It has much to offer if the plan is shared care. When parents cannot look after their disabled children full time, whether they are prevented by a care order or by their own situation, they will require permanent help. Substitute families can, if well prepared, offer the best permanent help, but it does not follow that the birth parents want to opt out. Much will depend on their ability and desire to remain parents, the carers' skills in balancing the needs of the child, the parents and their own; and on the level of support available from the agency. Shared care will work for the child if all the adults involved can co-operate and work in partnership.

It is also possible that potential permanent carers do not wish to take over the total responsibility for a child with complex disabilities. They might want to retain the support of the local authority – which is not as readily available for adopters – or require more financial help than an adoption allowance. Or they may simply not have the urge for legal recognition because they belong to a community where it is not the norm. This will also work for the child and for the the family, as long as it is not an expression of uncertainty about taking a child with disabilities or an indication that they will not consider themselves the child's permanent carers and advocates.

Adoption

Adoption is still the only sure way to secure legal permanence for children who cannot live with their families of origin. It provides a substitute family not only during childhood but for life; children with disabilities are likely to need that.

Some families are adopters by nature. They are ready to make a total commitment and to take on the whole responsibility; they want the disabled child to belong. This should not mean that they deny the birth parents, or the child's history, or that they do not celebrate adoption as a very different way of building a family. Openness in adoption, which may include direct contact with the birth family, is equally important for all children and can be very successful in placements of disabled children.[4]

Andrew and Gary are twelve-year-old twins who were known to the Social Services Department from a very young age because of concerns about serious neglect by their mother. She was already struggling to care for her two older children, partly because of her own background and partly due to her quite serious learning difficulties. The arrival of the twins stretched her capacities beyond her limits and the boys were given very little attention or care, and few boundaries. She seemed to be defeated by the task quite early on in their lives. As a result, they became wild and unmanageable. The family struggled on as best they could but eventually the boys came into care at their mother's request when they were ten years old.

They were placed with a foster family which provided excellent care and firm boundaries and both boys benefited enormously from this novel experience.

They blossomed and developed dramatically in the first six months and the progress continued through the next six months a little more slowly. They then reached a plateau, and their differing needs became obvious to the carers who began to find it difficult to manage both boys together. Some innate learning disabilities became more pronounced and the foster carers struggled with the lack of continuing progress.

The boys had not been recognised as disabled before being accommodated and no specialist disability services, such as respite, were built in to the placement. After 18 months, the carers and their family were nearly at breaking point and the placement disrupted. There was no other foster home available to meet Andrew and Gary's needs so they moved into the residential respite unit, where they still remain 18 months later.

The story of these boys and their contact with the local authority so far, illustrates a number of key points in the planning of services for children who are looked after.

The boys were not identified as having a disability until well over a year after they had been with foster carers. By that time the strain on the foster family was such that even with significant levels of respite, the placement broke down. It is likely that if the exceptional needs had been identified earlier, the placement would have been better supported from the beginning and may well have continued to meet Andrew and Gary's needs without wearing out the foster family.

Of course, in a case like this, it is always more difficult to disentangle the effects of emotional and social deprivation from those of a specific learning disability, but with skilled observation and assessment, input from psychologists, and listening to an experienced foster carer, it should be possible.

The lack of specialised residential provision is relevant to this case. The mainstream children's community homes would not meet the twins' needs, primarily because they have a population of teenagers with challenging behaviour, and it was felt that Andrew and Gary would be far too vulnerable. So the less detrimental alternative

– one of the respite units for children with disabilities – was chosen.

This has always been acknowledged as unsuitable on two counts: most of the other children have more severe disabilities, and the nature of respite care means the group is constantly changing, making it a very unsettling environment for these boys who need full-time care.

Policy questions arising out of this case are:
- Is it helpful to have the knowledge, expertise and skills about disability issues located in a division separate from mainstream child care services?
- Are there ways of making this specialist knowledge more available to an area worker picking up a case like Andrew and Gary's?
- Should the mainstream residential provision for children be more physically accessible and welcoming to disabled children? In other words, should we integrate disabled children into mainstream services?
- Would a more flexible and seamless approach to the range of respite, fostering, residential and shared care services have served these boys more effectively?
- Have they been discriminated against in service provision because of their impairments?

However, we are learning that some adopters who uncomplainingly walk more than the extra mile for their disabled children every day, and who in fact achieve seeming miracles, may not tolerate contact with birth families. As one adoptive mother put it: 'We've put all our energies, our love and our money into Kevin's progress – there's nothing left to spare. We never expected contact. We could only do what we did because he was our son.' If placements are made without setting up contact arrangements in advance, insurmountable barriers can soon be built; if contact is made a condition, some extraordinary adopters for children with disabilities may be lost.

In the late 1970s, adoption for disabled children was enthusiastically pursued for the first time. Older children who had languished in unsuitable residential homes were placed with families and unusual parents were found for unusual children. We widened our horizons without lowering our sights and refuted accusations of "second class families for second class children" with the evidence that it worked. It was thought that every child was adoptable. Indeed, every child surely *is* adoptable, but we do have to ask whether adoption is in the best interests of each and every child who needs a substitute family – disabled or not. At the same time we have to guard against allowing disabled children who are looked after by local authorities to be left behind because of financial considerations. It is expensive and time consuming to find, prepare and support adoptive parents, especially if enhanced adoption allowances are then paid – when local authorities are faced with dwindling budgets, disabled children do not have the loudest voice. Some specialist voluntary agencies will take referrals from local authorities to secure and maintain permanent family placements for children with disabilities (see Appendix E). This is not a cheaper option, but the purchase of a comprehensive package can offer a viable solution if social work time and expertise are under pressure.

Residential care

It may be that parents want residential care because they believe that only specialists can look after their disabled child, or it may be that it is the only way to meet all of a child's needs. Residential care for disabled children is not the undesirable option it is often made out to be; it is the lack of planning and purpose which are undesirable. Indeed, at best, residential care can offer much and can be the placement of choice for some children.

At worst, it may be that children with disabilities are placed in unsuitable residential care because there is nothing else available and that they are left there because no-one is complaining or asking the right questions.

Derek who developed tuberous sclerosis as an infant, was placed in a home for children with disabilities, at his parents' request, when he was three years old. He was the baby in the home, he enjoyed a great deal of attention, and it was supposed that he would stay there until he was 18, when he would have to move on. The parents visited regularly at first, then less and less frequently. By the time Derek was ten years old, contact with his family had petered out. His parents had divorced, his mother had remarried, and his father had gone to work in the Middle East. There were no siblings or other interested relatives.

Derek was no longer the youngest child in the home and had become more physically and mentally disabled by his progressive illness. The home, which had never been selected as particularly appropriate for Derek, but had offered a benign caretaking facility, was being re-organised to take young adults in semi-independent units.

An arbitrary decision was made to place all the children with families. In spite of rigorous efforts by a competent fostering and adoption section, Derek was the only child left in the home two years later. Introductions to an experienced adoptive family had failed and caused distress to Derek, the family, the staff at the home and the social workers. Finally, an independent consultant recommended that Derek, now nearly 13, should be placed in a residential home, which should be as carefully assessed to meet his present and long-term needs as any family would be.

Coming to this post from a background of adoption and fostering work, I was well aware of the gaps in my knowledge about disability and also spent the first three months trying to immerse myself in the world of disabled children and their families.

I built up a picture of their particular concerns and how services currently provided in Bradford are helpful or unhelpful in meeting their needs. A number of themes emerged which I noted in my diary.

17 March 95 I can identify issues, but resolving questions such as whether or not to develop integrated residential care for disabled and non disabled children has to be tackled at a higher level. While there is no-one with joint responsibility for strategic planning for disabled children below Director level, it seems unlikely that there will be a resolution. In the absence of an overview, services cannot be developed in an interlocking way to provide the continuum of care that is needed for children like Andrew and Gary. At the meeting of the Steering Group for my post today, we discussed the problem of the lack of adequate full-time residential provision for disabled children in the department. It was agreed that it needed some attention and the Area Manager from the Disability Division promised to talk to one of the Area Managers in the Children's Division to try to put some strategic planning in place.

4 April 95 Disabled children and their families do not have "special needs". Their needs are the same as everyone else's, but society is organised in such a way as to place enormous obstacles to getting those needs met, because the delivery has to be more specialised.

Parents of disabled children, in order to survive this obstacle course, need to develop a wide range of additional skills in negotiating, advocating, organising, understanding bureaucracy, fighting for services and winkling out information which is not made easily available. This has clear implications for what we might need to look for in substitute families.

Most families of even profoundly and multiply disabled children are "hanging on in there", committed to caring for their children and getting the best for them, with the odds often stacked against them.

Most parents, while welcoming occasional breaks from caring for their disabled children (like most other parents) are, at least initially, highly suspicious of this provision if it is labelled as "fostering", whereas the words "respite" and "shared care" do not hold such negative connotations for them.

Residential care often seems more secure to many parents who come to depend on respite services – they can count on a building always being there, with staff who are paid to do a job. In contrast, family based provision can seem more insecure and too dependent on the goodwill of the family offering the service.

Most children do not come into care solely, or even primarily, because of their impairment. Parental isolation, serious mental or physical ill health, "care histories" of their own, current drug or alcohol abuse, or domestic violence, often result in problems of family breakdown, neglect and abuse. Of course, the extra demands on these parents caused by disability will have exacerbated the problems, and while they may already be struggling with the considerable demands of "ordinary" parenting, it is not surprising that they cannot find the energy and stamina that parents of disabled children need.

It is easy to see why, traditionally, services for disabled children and their families have been seen as discrete and separate from mainstream child care provision. In Bradford, there was, and remains, a strong lobby to keep the services separate so as to ring fence at least some resources specifically for the problems which arise purely from a child's impairment. Otherwise, it is argued, these needs will be overshadowed and swamped by mainstream child care, particularly child protection work.

A group home for disabled teenagers was found, which had links with higher special education and was part of a larger community. Derek could remain permanently and there would be various occupational opportunities.

Possibly the right residential care would always have been the placement of choice for Derek, but aimless care of any kind can only make one handicap too many.[5]

Conclusion

The range of substitute care for children with disabilities must be responsive to changing needs and offer a comprehensive, flexible service; a service parents, children and all kinds of carers want, can use, understand and participate in. It is vital to assess what is needed and to define what is offered.

Parents who cannot look after their disabled children do not usually want to sever links with their children and they retain parental responsibility unless their children are adopted. Contact, shared care and openness in adoption are always sensitive issues, but I have found that there can be added complexities when disability is directly or indirectly the reason for separation.

Finally, children with disabilities require the best of the same services as *all* children who are separated from their own families. Should we therefore create special services for disabled children or should we develop existing services to be good enough for all children, including those with disabilities? Does departmental policy encourage integration or segregation? How are the interests of children with disabilities served in the Children's Services Plans?

Ailie Kerrane describes how one local authority serves families and their disabled children who require placements outside the home.

References

1. Baldwin S, *The Cost of Caring: Families with disabled children*, Routledge and Kegan Paul, 1985.
2. Beresford B, *Expert Opinions: A national survey of parents caring for a severely disabled child*, Joseph Rowntree Foundation / Community Care, Bristol Policy Press, 1995
3. Department of Health, *Children Act Guidance & Regulations, Vol.6, Children with Disabilities*, HMSO, 1991.
4. Fratter J, *Adoption with Contact: Implications for policy and practice*, BAAF, 1996.
5. Russell P, *Children with Disabilities: Some current issues*, National Children's Bureau, 1993.

1 May 95 In this post, with "a foot in both camps", I have found two distinct and very different cultures. I will exaggerate to underline the differences:

DISABILITY CARE PROVISION	MAINSTREAM CHILD CARE PROVISION
deserving families	undeserving families
parent centred	child centred
parents strongly valued	parents under suspicion
working in partnership	investigation
involving parents in plans	legal intervention

Although this polarises attitudes in an extreme, unrealistic and unhelpful way, there are grains of truth here which I find helpful in understanding some of the obstacles which have historically prevented services from developing in a coherent and integrated way. The necessarily rigorous approach to child protection can seem to clash with the more apparently sympathetic approach to disability. There still remains a mutual suspicion, although inroads have been made in breaking down barriers and each service has gained understanding and insight from the other's perspective.

If we are to provide a flexible range of services which meet the needs of disabled children and their families right through the spectrum from respite to adoption, then we must continue this dialogue at all levels of the service.

Is a family which needs occasional respite different in kind from a family which is at breaking point because of problems like isolation or physical abuse? I believe that answering "yes" to that question leads to separation of services and danger of the kind of polarisation I have outlined above. If it is "no", then we must see each child

and family as a unique blend of strengths and weaknesses and work wholeheartedly to build on the strengths, mobilising all possible resources to ensure quality and continuity of care for the child.

This would include allowing parents to relinquish caring for their child on a part or full-time basis, and grasping the nettle where legal action has to be taken to secure the protection of a child. It is possible to intervene in children's lives in a way which places their needs first, and respects the worth and value of their parents without either patronising or punishing them.

SECTION TWO

Finding and recruiting substitute families

Who's for families?

There is an alternative family somewhere for every child – if we haven't found it, we haven't looked hard enough. This is not a glib catch phrase or a rosy view of child care, but a considered opinion based on experience of finding families for children who used to be described as the most "hard to place". What that same experience must lead us to ask is: 'Yes, but can every child use a family?' and 'Is it always preferable to live in a family, even for a limited period?' and 'What is a family for? – to offer respite, shared or permanent care?'

Margery was referred to a specialist adoption agency. She was 12 years old and had been brought up in a children's home almost from birth. Her mother was admitted as a long-term patient to a psychiatric hospital soon after Margery was born; there was never any contact.

Margery had cerebral palsy and was partially sighted. She could not walk unaided, she had a severe speech impairment and learning difficulties. She was also a cheerful and affectionate child who loved outings and treats. The staff at the children's home had remained unusually constant and there were two other children with disabilities who had grown up in the same group and went to the same special school as Margery. Family placement had not been recommended for any one of these three children until the home was forced to close down.

It was surprisingly easy to find a family who wanted Margery: a young couple with two school-age children and a wealth of professional experience in cerebral palsy. But Margery was not the child they expected, in spite of knowing all there was to know about her. When they withdrew soon after

introductions began, a second family came forward.

These parents had enjoyed bringing up two children of their own with cerebral palsy and were eager to share their lives and their suitably equipped home with another disabled child. This time the introductions went from good to better, and Margery moved in happily enough and as well prepared for the change as possible. At first, the excitement of her new surroundings and the concentrated attention from her new family was enough to make the placement work for her. The parents expected the honeymoon period to give way to more challenging behaviour, but they were taken aback by the deep depression which set in. Margery became listless, she lost her normally large appetite, she refused to join the family in any activity and she became almost mute. Her new school queried whether she was sick. Yet she came to life whenever there was a phone call or a visit from the children's home. At Christmas, she refused to buy presents for anyone except her two friends in the home. The wise parents concluded that Margery was mourning the loss of the only "family" she knew – a family that had sustained her for twelve years; if she had missed out on anything, she was unaware of it.

Margery went back to her children's home after four months. In due course, potential adopters were found for her two friends with very similar outcomes. In the end, an enlightened local authority agreed not to split the "family" more than the circumstances dictated.

An ordinary council house was allocated to the three children. They became the tenants and the Director of Social Services acted on their behalf. An older couple with their own disabled teenage son was recruited to move in with the children, instead of the other way round. And because the house was in the same area as the children's home, the retiring staff could stay connected and the children could remain at the same school.

Margery and her friends could not join a family because they were not able to conceptualise or to make any kind of investment in having a mother and a father in preference to devoted staff and each other. Their eagerness to have a family of their own had been on a simple storybook level, like listening to *The Three Little Bears* and having a treat and an outing all rolled into one. Other disabled children might have taken the leap into the unknown and, with the right support, might have become members of a more conventional family, but these three children could not go so far. They related to the carers who moved in with them, as they had related to staff at the children's home, and they were content.

Fifteen-year-old Allen, who was quadriplegic and unable to speak or do anything at all for himself, had also been in an institution since birth; but he moved easily into his one-parent family and blossomed against every prediction and prognosis. He did not learn to talk or to walk, but he did respond to the total commitment of one person and learned to smile and to demonstrate delight and a will of his own.

As with all children, it is a question of assessing attachments and the capacity for extending attachments. Allen had made no attachments in his residential home; he might not have been able to attach to his substitute parent, but he did. Margery had made strong attachments but unlike more able children, she could not extend or transfer them to a new family.

Some knowledge of attachment theory is essential in all placement work.[1] When children are disabled it may be more difficult to read the signals correctly.

13 February 95 Generally familiarising myself with the work of the team for children with disabilities and their families. Will attend one of their team meetings soon. Concerns seem to be about boundaries between their team and the constituency Children's Teams.

A worker I spoke to about my post (who was involved in the initial exploratory project) had a clear view of the role – co-ordination, bridge-building, empowerment, and identifying existing skills and resources, rather than primarily for the recruitment of families. But I do need to think about how to adapt mainstream methods and knowledge of recruitment, preparation, assessment, training and support of carers, to the specific task of caring for a disabled child.

O NE of the first issues I have to address in this post is whether to recommend that a small specialist section within the Adoption and Fostering Unit should take on this work.

Some of the most helpful information about current practice was in the original report completed prior to my appointment. The workers interviewed a cross-section of carers who were looking after disabled children to find out what their views of the service were. The collected responses of the carers are outlined below in question and answer form.

1. Did the carer have full details of the disability prior to placement?

Sometimes the amount of information given varied according to the length of the matching process; for instance, when young people were placed at a time of crisis, there were some very basic omissions in terms of medical detail. One set of carers said they only learned of the young person's condition in "dribs and drabs". Other carers, whilst fully conversant with the young person's condition, were not fully prepared for the long-term needs.

In conclusion, most carers felt that they were reasonably well informed about current medical/physical conditions but not about the changing and often increasing complexity of long-term needs. The more experienced carers became, the better able they were to ask the appropriate questions needed to gather the right information.

Allen remained with his foster carer for three years. Then he became too heavy for one person to manage and as his disabilities progressed, he needed nursing care. His carer fought for the most appropriate residential provision and remained his family for the rest of his short life. Allen died when he was twenty one. Although his experience of family was so brief, would anyone suggest that it had not been worthwhile?

Who chooses to have disabled children?

However long or short substitute family care is to be, whether it be temporary or permanent, regular or spasmodic, conventional or innovative, nothing can be done unless families are recruited.

It is sometimes suggested that there must be something odd about people who deliberately take on the care of a child with disabilities. Parents of disabled children are suspicious about their motives, residential workers are dubious about their stamina, and even family placement workers are uncertain about their ability to do what they say they want to do.

There are people who begin by wanting to adopt or foster an ordinary child and then stretch to meet a greater need. But more often, families choose to have a disabled child because they know about disability; or they already have a disabled child, sibling or other relative; or they have worked with disabled people or they know and like the disabled old lady down the road.

Margaret became a teacher for deaf children after her own daughter was born deaf. When her daughter left home to get married, Margaret looked around for a deaf teenager in care who needed a family. She responded to publicity about two profoundly deaf sisters and eventually adopted them both.

People like Margaret want children because of, and not in spite of, their disabilities.

The Whites had a son, Brian, who was four years old and had Down's Syndrome. They wanted a second child, but they were so delighted with Brian that they decided to have another baby with Down's Syndrome. They adopted Henry and two years later they added Paul – also a child with Down's Syndrome – to their family.

Prospective carers who are themselves disabled can offer a unique role model, insight and expertise, if the child's needs match what they have to give. But the child's needs must always come first, and no-one, including a person with disabilities, has a right to a child.

Ethel was born with a syndrome which stunted her growth. She was barely four feet tall. Her husband, Ralph, was partially sighted. They adopted a baby with an undiagnosed set of disabilities and an uncertain prognosis. Later an older girl with achondroplasia (dwarfism) joined the family. Both children flourished with their disabled parents and grew up to value themselves as young people with disabilities.

Some families, who have brought up several children of their own successfully, say that they want to go on being parents but are ready to do something more challenging than ordinary parenting.

When the last of Sheilagh and Ben's three children left home, they decided that they liked nothing as much as being active parents. They heard of a baby with a fatal heart condition who needed a family to nurture him until he died. Sheilagh and Ben fostered the baby while he had a series of operations. He survived with brain damage and stayed permanently with Sheilagh and Ben. Next came an eleven-year-old girl who had been abused and consequently had severe learning difficulties. She was followed by a hyperactive boy with epilepsy. And so it went on. When the family was rehoused to give them more space, they took more children. When Ben was made redundant, he became a full-time foster father.

2. Which factors influenced the carer's decision to offer a placement to a young person with special needs?

"A child needs a home" was the response of some experienced link carers who felt they would accept most young people needing a placement irrespective of whether they had a disability or not.

Other carers had more personal reasons – often relating to their own history – for offering a placement to a child with disabilities. Some were motivated by family or work experience either in a nursing or residential setting. These carers felt they had both confidence and expertise to offer. In spite of the potential complications of the care task, including hospitalisation and frequent checks on health and/or constant supervision, they felt confident about handling the young person and effecting a general improvement in the quality of their life.

The family composition and expressed views of other family members also affected the decision to offer a placement to a child with disabilities, as it does in fostering generally. Some carers had thought of offering these specialised placements for some time, even years, but only came forward following a change in family composition.

Some were initially recruited as respite carers – they could sympathise with the parents' need for an occasional break. As they became more experienced, they gained the confidence to offer a long-term placement.

One family had been matched with a young person who subsequently became profoundly disabled – they felt their commitment to him remained unchanged.

A number of carers expressed ideological reasons for fostering disabled children: a recognition that disability could happen to any of us, the resulting injustice and stigma in terms of society's changed response to the person, and, as one carer said, a desire to help someone who had 'no choices'.

3. Were difficulties generated for the carers by fostering a child or young person with disabilities?

Depending on the degree and type of disability, all the carers have had to adapt the way in which their family life is organised. For one family, any venture away from home takes more than an hour's preparation.

Most carers have had to make changes in terms of reducing hours or giving up paid work outside the home, and there have been inevitable restrictions on planning outings and holidays which have caused problems for the birth children in the foster home and for other family members.

There were a number of other practical difficulties relating to the carers' perceived lack of specialist support, training, and provision of aids and adaptations. Some said that social workers have limited further placements of children they wished to foster.

Most of these carers have very real concerns for the long-term future of the young people they foster: who will care for them as adults? Could they themselves shoulder the financial burden of changing status from foster to adult carer? They also expressed concerns about outliving the young person and the stress of fostering a child when the prognosis is poor.

Several carers felt that having to seek information rather than being given it, was belittling and disempowering.

Carers fostering a young person with either a physical impairment or a learning difficulty were often restricted, more than other carers, in their use of "babysitters".

In conclusion, there was a consensus that there are many additional difficulties generated by fostering a young person with a disability. The carers were also unanimous in stating that they got a lot out of their fostering experiences and that there were rewards to be gained from specialised caring.

4. Which specific supports would help carers?

– provision of ongoing training and support;
– specialist workers from the Adoption and Fostering Unit to provide guidance regarding appropriate resources and channels of support;
– telephone lines for emergency/crisis support;
– carers' support groups;
– regular provision of information from Social Services rather than carers having to take responsibility for searching out the information;
– regular respite – also overnight and "babysitting" respite;

Many people find the inner strength and motivation to offer something extra through their religion. A few, who consider themselves to be disadvantaged by their own life experiences or by social conventions, have a deep sympathy for children they see as being disabled by their impairment: women who have been sexually abused, lesbian and gay couples and people who have grown up in care, have all made good alternative parents for children with disabilities. What they have had in common with other successful substitute families is a proven ability to overcome problems, which is a more positive indicator than a trouble-free life. Other qualities they share are a willingness to adjust to changing circumstances, openness, the ability to communicate and stand up to criticism, and to fight for their rights.

On the other hand, there are some qualities which, in general, are warning signals: rigid attitudes or constant anger towards authority, social isolation, fear of being labelled, and secrets in the family. It would be as mistaken to advocate that all gay people or all Jehovah's Witnesses make good carers, as it would be to discriminate against them.

All sorts of people make families for all sorts of children. Single people can give one-to-one attention, which many disabled children need, without neglecting anyone else; divorced or remarried people and members of all kinds of minority groups could be the right substitute family for a specific child, and they may have the strength to go the extra mile for a disabled child.

Members of minority ethnic groups who are under-represented as carers of children with disabilities, would surely come forward more readily if a higher value was put on what they have to offer. They should be made aware of how needed they are, how welcomed they would be and how much support they would have.

Publicity and recruitment

No-one simply wakes up any morning of the week and decides to foster or to adopt or to offer respite care to a child with disabilities, unless the need is made known. Some agencies still talk of "advertising" their children. There is nothing wrong with the true meaning of that word, but it has become corrupted by marketing techniques, and we do not want to suggest that we are trading children. Parents often express aversion to any hint of advertising but are more amenable to discussing publicity for their child.

Eva, a mother no longer able to look after her autistic daughter, Heather, had asked the local authority to accommodate her in a residential home until they could find foster carers for her. A keen worker telephoned the mother in the evening and asked for permission to advertise Heather in a national newspaper; she was in a hurry to meet a deadline for a "special offer" from the paper. Eva was horrified and refused. The worker, who was properly determined to find a home for Heather, said the mother was unreasonable and unco-operative and the department should seek a care order to protect the placement plans. Her line manager, who had never met Eva, consulted with the legal department; the advice was that if a parent obstructs the agreed child care plans, then the child could be at risk of significant harm and the local authority could apply for a care order. So Eva was faced with a harsh ultimatum: agree to advertising or the department would apply for a care order.

This particular situation was satisfactorily resolved when another worker intervened. She explained why Heather needed publicity rather than advertising, she and Eva discussed what kind of publicity would be best, they devised a text to describe Heather and why she needed foster care, and they explored how Eva might deal with comments from people who saw the publicity. Eva now felt that she was making it possible for Heather to have the best chance of getting the right family, whereas she had previously felt punished for wanting to have her fostered at all.

– information on benefits, allowances and grants automatically given out and regularly updated;
– a more consistent system of payments (an ad hoc system can create resentment among carers);
– practical help to apply for benefits;
– information about specialist voluntary organisations;
– confidence building courses to help carers work more assertively alongside health professionals;
– assistance in creating a network of local carers;
– assistance in applying for aids and adaptations;
– involvement of, for example, a district nurse or someone with medical knowledge;
– home helps.

5. How best to recruit carers for young people with disabilities?

Carers thought that confidence in enabling and helping young people with disabilities grew alongside experience.

Most of the group had become carers of children with disabilities by default or because they had worked with or known a disabled young person in their family or amongst friends. Hence, there was enthusiasm for recruiting by word of mouth, particularly for specialist schemes. There was a belief that ignorance and fear about disability have prevented potential applicants from coming forward.

Carers who were matched with a young person who subsequently became disabled, felt disability was an unknown quantity for the general public and many people would not come forward in answer to an advertisement. General education regarding disability should accompany any attempts to recruit.

Other ideas related to the recruitment of foster carers generally:
– sending a newsletter to existing carers;
– using BAAF child placement services;
– posting publicity in local shops, launderettes, etc.

A number of carers felt that financial incentives might enable people to provide care as a full time form of employment. In addition, publicising help available with adaptations could encourage people to come forward who may have expected to be excluded on grounds of unsuitable accommodation.

6. Are there problems regarding finance, aids and adaptations?

There was a general view that financial responsibility for young people with disabilities was greater in respect of special diets, wear and tear on clothing, nappies, bedding, aids, transport and other related matters.

The carers did not necessarily feel that they incurred any greater costs themselves because there were various grants to cover additional expenses. Information about grants and benefits and the financing of adaptations to property was vitally important for all.

Acting on the results

Building on the foundations of these findings and recommendations, I started to tackle as many of the issues identified as possible.

My main strategy in this process has been the setting up of a group for carers with a particular interest in children with disabilities. There are 40 households on the mailing list – a much smaller number attend each meeting, but everyone receives any relevant information about services, training or other items of interest.

The group is used for information sharing, discussion of topics of mutual interest, and as a sounding board for ideas. At the first meeting I wanted some feedback about possible specialisation of the work with children with disabilities. I was given a very clear message that it would not be popular among this group of carers. For example, many of the link carers – ie. those offering bridging placements for children who will go home or on to a permanent substitute family – like to absorb one child with disabilities into their family while providing another placement for a child without. They felt strongly that this gave the child with disabilities a much more integrated and "ordinary" experience of family life. It also gave the carers and their families a continuing broad range of fostering experience. From a worker's perspective, the non-specialist approach provides a potentially large pool of carers when looking for a placement. For example, recently we were asked to find a three week placement for a disabled brother and sister while their mother went into hospital. They both had significant disabilities and needed a high level of care and supervision.

Ironically, Heather was eventually featured in the same national paper which had offered to "advertise" her in the first place. A full length article about foster care and adoption included a photograph and details about Heather. One family responded: one family is enough if it is the right one, and it was.

Features in newspapers and magazines usually create more interest than straightforward appeals in the advertising columns, and they come free. They also remove the item from any connection with advertisements. There is a place for advertisements of course, for instance, to recruit respite or short-term foster carers in general; when the focus is on the *job* and not on the child. But even then, a feature in a magazine will lie around a dentist's waiting room long after a newspaper has been thrown away.

It is useful for family placement teams to cultivate links with local reporters and radio stations; or failing that, to develop skills in writing short features which the paper may be pleased to publish – there could even be a small fee paid to the agency for a change. A regular spot about children who need families usually draws a good response and raises awareness of disability in the community; letters to suitably targeted magazines, like the *Farmer's Weekly*, can have surprising results and reach a fresh audience.

Dear Editor,

We thought that some of your readers might like to hear about Liam. He is nearly five years old and is looking forward to his birthday party. Liam is an unusual child because he was born with Noonan Syndrome, a rare condition which means that he will always be very small and have a distinctive appearance. Liam goes to a special school for children with learning difficulties where he is one of the most able pupils. He is a great chatterer but it is sometimes difficult to understand him; he is having speech therapy and tries hard to speak more slowly and clearly.

Although Liam is generally healthy, he is prone to get serious chest infections in polluted air; he hates being ill and dreams of living in the country. He says that he wants to be a farmer when he grows up. He loves animals and is gentle with small creatures. Liam has lived in a home for disabled children since he was a baby. His parents are divorced and have never had a stable home. His mother has visited him regularly and hoped to be able to look after him, but she now wants him to have a better life than she could offer. She has asked us to find him a permanent family and would be willing to agree to adoption. She hopes that she will be able to keep in touch with her son. Liam's father also wants him to have a family; he moves around and occasionally sends postcards to Liam which he treasures. It will be important for Liam to continue to have contact with his parents. A fostering or adoption allowance will be payable.

Liam has helped to write this letter and says that he wants families to know that he is a faddy eater but loves chips and lots of gravy.

If any of your readers would like to know more about Liam, and live no further than a three hour journey from Birmingham, we would be very pleased to hear from them.

It is clearly easier and more enjoyable for everyone involved, especially if the child is able to participate, to write a brief story without the limitations and format of an advertisement.

Photolisting services to find permanent families, such as *Be my Parent* and *Focus on Fives* (both published by BAAF)[2] and *Adoption UK*[3] as well as *BAAFLink*, a computerised nationwide family finding service, may lead to interagency placements. These are relatively cheap to use if they attract approved families, as they often do; but there is a tendency for children who have complex disabling conditions to be left behind. However, it is not always predictable which child will have to wait longest for a placement.

Three infants with Down's syndrome were referred for adoption at the same time to an agency which runs its own photosheet mailing list. Two of the babies were healthy and looked appealing; the third was premature, had a heart condition, and a noticeable

squint. The ailing child was placed first. When asked why they had chosen him, the prospective adopters said: 'He wanted a family most.'

Age is generally a more serious barrier for family placement than the most severe disability, but again, it need not be so every time.

A fifteen-year-old girl with cystic fibrosis and a short life expectancy was placed with a woman in her early sixties. She was "chosen" as soon as the first item of publicity appeared in the newsletter circulated by a self-help society concerned with that particular disability. The woman who applied had been dreaming of such an opportunity ever since she retired from working in a children's hospital, but had never done anything about it until she saw the newsletter.

Interest group newsletters and magazines offer excellent opportunities to publicise specific children, but most children for whom a family may be difficult to find, must have more widespread and intensive publicity.

Jason was a black African toddler with Smith Magenis syndrome, a condition giving rise to varying severe disabilities and therefore often left undiagnosed. He was referred for permanent placement to a specialist agency with one African-Caribbean and three white workers, all determined to find African carers for Jason. They used newspapers with a significant African readership to publicise Jason, and they sought advice from African workers and appointed one to act as a consultant. They made themselves familiar with Jason's background. They learnt about his country, his culture, his religion and his language. They went to speak in a church where members of the congregation came from the same country, and they finally found a single parent from a different African country who was as eager to learn about Jason's background as they had been. What drew her to Jason was the specific nature of the publicity which acknowledged and respected who he was.

One of our link families who had no previous experience of disability accepted the placement and enjoyed the experience. They were glad it was only three weeks because it was very hard work but it has introduced them to a different kind of caring and stretched their capabilities. Many of our carers currently looking after children with disabilities started by chance, enjoyed it and went on to take more children with disabilities. One danger of specialisation would be to lose that kind of growth and the resulting flexibility.

Although the carers in the group were against total specialisation, they would welcome:
– a specialist worker within the Unit;
– up-to-date training and information on disability;
– opportunities to meet with other carers of disabled children.

Having established this bimonthly group, my recommendation to the Department was not to set up a separate, specialist section, but to improve the services to children with disabilities and their carers within the Fostering and Adoption Unit. I will also recommend the establishment of a worker to specialise in disability issues, and to provide a link with the Disability Division.

I learned about many more issues facing both adopters and foster carers, from a number of visits to different carers in the early days of the job.

16 May 95 Visited Jim and Mary Mitchell. They were community foster carers whose foster child, Steve, suddenly became very ill and then severely disabled as a result of the illness. They saw him through the illness and subsequent disability and were committed to keeping him on a long-term basis. But sadly Steve died about six months ago and they are now committed to taking on another child with severe disabilities. They talked at length and very movingly about caring for Steve – they are obviously still in the midst of mourning for him. They seem to grieve much the same as any parents for their lost child, but perhaps with less devastation. I found it impossible to know whether the timing of thinking about another child was right or not. With birth parents, or adopters, I would normally have a "rule of thumb" that they should allow themselves at least a full first year of the grieving process before parenting another child. Is it so different for foster carers? They certainly still seemed very preoccupied with Steve and his death.

Ideally, each time a child or an identified group of children is referred for substitute family care, publicity should be specially designed to find the families for them. Time and again children wait for respite care, foster care or adoption because no-one suitable has been found in various "pools" of approved families. Although most people can become the right parents for some child, hardly anyone can become the right parent for any child. To be approved for a physically disabled child between the ages of five and ten makes little sense when we know the variation in range and degree of disabilities. Far better allow people to respond to a real child and then prepare them and approve them to take care of that child. And a real child must always have a real name; many families have been dismayed to find that Alice, whose story and photograph appeared in the paper, is really Avril. Names play an important part in our lives: they belong to the chemistry of attraction.

Projects and campaigns

It is often more productive, as well as more economical, to work with a group of children and to devise publicity which will feature every individual child while focusing interest on the group.

> *In a rural area, the parents of five children with severe learning difficulties asked the local authority to set up a family link scheme for respite care. After an unsuccessful attempt to use some of their short-term foster carers, the family placement team, working closely with the children's parents and social workers, co-ordinated a local campaign to find a new family for each child. Leaflets explaining the need for respite care, the aims of a link scheme and pen pictures of the five children were circulated to health centres, libraries and churches in the area. The parents and workers, with some help from the children, made decorative posters together about each child. They used bright colours, bold writing, clear photographs and had fun. They stuck the posters up on the wall of a social services training room, and held a well-publicised open meeting. The social workers gave out*

> *information about the department, the responsibilities of respite carers and the process of becoming approved. The parents came to answer questions about their children and to serve coffee and cakes after the meeting.*

> *Twenty people attended – eight couples and four single women. Four of the couples and three of the single women said they would like to follow up with an interview. After two months of preparatory work, mostly as a group, the three single women and two couples were linked with the five children and their parents.*

Similar campaigns can be designed specifically for black disabled children or for other groups of children needing different family care. Projects to place several children can generate new energy among workers; combining parents, children and carers at an early stage could be the beginning of a mutual support network. It is best to limit such projects to children who have something in common, so that the publicity, and later the group work, can have a shared theme; for instance, children with Down's Syndrome of varying ages, infants with severe congenital abnormalities, older children who have spent years in institutions, children with restricted mobility, and as many other categories as seem practicable and appropriate. The desired form of care should also be the same for each child in the group and clearly stated, but it would be a mistake to be too prescriptive so early on; the idea is not to mislead, but to encourage everyone who might have anything to offer to make further enquiries.

What do substitute families have a right to expect?

This is a better question to ask than "How do we assess families?" and can be more simply answered.

Information and explanation

Families who pursue publicity regarding specific children or recruitment for specific services, require information.

They need to know about the agency: how does it function, who is in charge, what are the procedures, what are the choices, what financial rewards exist, if any, how long will it take, and are there any set criteria?

They then require information about the child they are interested in: what exactly does the disability mean for this child's day-to-day living, is there a prognosis, is treatment available, does the child attend a special school, and does he or she have contact with parents, siblings or other family members?

They should be informed about services and benefits for disabled children in general, about the reasons for having respite care, about the difference between long and short-term foster care and adoption.

They should know how decisions will be made, who will make them, and what they can do if they disagree.

The first tentative queries will almost always be made on the telephone. Much will therefore depend on who answers the phone, how the caller is received, and how soon a full information pack is sent. Publicity should always be accompanied by an immediately available information pack. Some agencies prefer to give out initial information at private interviews, others at open meetings to which all first enquirers are invited. They will not all be able to come, and several will have a change of heart between telephoning and taking the next step; but no matter, the most determined will make it and the rest may come back another time if they were made to feel welcome.

Derek and Joan, a childless couple in their late forties, saw an article in a magazine about a little girl of four with spina bifida. They phoned the agency, had a friendly chat and said they would love to come to an open meeting. They had to travel to London from the Midlands and when they arrived at Euston they got cold feet about the whole thing. They turned back and went home.

Jim and Mary want to use this experience productively and are keen to apply the knowledge of disability they gained through Steve to benefit other young people. On a practical level, they also have all the adaptations and equipment to care for a profoundly disabled person.

13 June 95 *Visited Valerie Sanders. Val has fostered many children, but her experience of caring for Andrew and Gary, the twins with learning disabilities, was one of the most difficult, and nearly led to the family giving up fostering. She has also adopted a child with a disability.*

Talked in some detail about living with Andrew and Gary. They were placed with her in the summer holidays and it was only when the boys went back to school and the teachers asked where Gary's hearing aid was that Val knew anything about his hearing impairment. This points to how crucial it is to ensure that accurate and full information is given to carers from the beginning. This is not as simple as it sounds, because significant information is often scattered around and not gathered neatly in one place. Parents might be the only people who have access to all the relevant information, but, as in this case, their lives are chaotic, or they may have very limited ability to understand and process the information themselves. So a crucial task in any placement, particularly an emergency one, is to locate the relevant information and pass it on to the foster carers.

Could I have a role in this? Partly it could be covered in a training session, but it is not always possible to target the right workers. Anyone in the Department could be in this key position and sometimes no one seems to know about a particular child's disability. But at least I could help to raise awareness of this. We also talked about the kind of help and information needed by adoptive parents who do not have the counselling and information sessions afforded to parents who give birth to a disabled child. This gap could be filled by ensuring that any adoptive parent is given very detailed information and easy access to experts such as psychologists or doctors.

The next day they looked at the article once more and decided they couldn't leave it. So they rang again and asked if they could have a private interview. This time they not only made it to the agency but, armed with all the information they could wish for, they went on to the next stage and the next, and adopted the little girl with spina bifida six months later.

Good and sufficient information early on not only encourages people to proceed, it also enables them to withdraw before they go too far for comfort.

Activity days

It is notoriously difficult to describe children and even more difficult to describe children with disabilities. Two families can have entirely different reactions to the same child and perceive entirely different problems stemming from the same disability.

Gloria had no speech, was in a wheelchair and could not do anything for herself. She was honestly described in the publicity. When a prospective carer saw her, she said: 'You didn't tell me she was so peaceful.'

One way of sharing information is to let children speak for themselves. This is straightforward when it is a matter of respite care or planned short-term foster care. If children are being looked after by the local authority and need permanent families, it is common practice now to show videos before families commit themselves, but it is more tricky to arrange actual meetings. It is not acceptable to have children "looked over", and "blind viewings" incline towards a cloak and dagger approach. It is possible, however, to organise an outing for a group of children who need families, and to prepare a group of families to join the children in a day of activities.

These activities may involve nothing more than playing in a soft environment, sharing meals, going for a walk and keeping tired children occupied. Clearly, only children who would not be disturbed by the experience should be included in activity days.

Seven-year-old Jasmine was quite unperturbed when it was explained to her that she had already met her new parents at the activity day. She could remember nothing about it; one day was much like another to Jasmine who had sustained serious brain damage during an operation to remove a tumour. But when she saw them again, three months later, she seemed to recognise something about them and she said 'I like you'. Her new family reported that the experience of spending a day with Jasmine, of feeding, toileting, pushing the wheelchair through a crowded shopping area and trying to amuse her, had taught them more in six hours than reading four volumes of files.

Information has no end. There is no point at which giving information stops and something else in the assessment takes its place. Information is the accompaniment at every stage and the quality of information can make or mar a placement. But the timing is as important as the quality. We all know the feeling of trying to absorb information when we are not ready for it.

I am writing this in a foreign country. I read the travel guides before I came, I was interested, but I could not relate to the information and I did not absorb it. Now that I am here, now that I can see the sights, I want to learn more and more about the place and I retain the information.

It is the same with family placement; information will have to be reissued for families in step with progress, just as it has to be recycled for children to fit their stage of development and comprehension.

Long-term foster carers of a ten-year-old boy with partial sight and a hearing loss, who were shown the child's file before placement, were confused by the wealth of detailed recordings and expert opinions. After the child had been with them for a month, they asked to read the file again. This time they knew what to look for.

Recruitment

Children referred to me presented me with a challenge in terms of their own needs and levels of impairment and the kind of family placements they required.

Although I initially resisted the idea of becoming actively involved in recruitment of families – because the post was temporary and I was aware of the need for continuity and support for carers – I have become responsible for a new piece of recruitment work on the understanding that the children's own social workers will take on the post-placement support. If the pilot project is successful, I hope that the Department might go on to develop a scheme with adequate social work support built in.

This project concerns 12-year-old Peter who has Down's Syndrome, and 10-year-old Rosie who has Rett Syndrome. The following diary entries chart the course of piloting a shared care scheme prompted by the needs of these two children.

4 April 95 Meeting with Bob, Peter's social worker. Peter currently lives half the week with his mother and the other half in the residential respite unit. This is a stable arrangement which is working well; it enables his mother to continue caring for him. But there are significant problems in the residential unit because Peter often displays aggressive behaviour towards the younger or more vulnerable children in the unit. He also seems to target certain staff members with similar behaviour, like biting and kicking, when he is not getting individual attention. His behaviour is not so difficult at home where he appears to be much happier and more settled, and where there is no competition! Bob is keen to find a family alternative for this shared care arrangement. Peter's mother is also keen. Said I would check all possible "in house" resources with the Adoption and Fostering Unit and respite care scheme during the next week. If there is nothing (which I suspect will be the case), then we'll look at other possibilities. Perhaps take on a piece of specific recruitment through publicity? Consider developing a shared care scheme?

5 April 95 Visit to Leeds Social Services Department to look at their scheme for long-term placements of disabled children. This operates as a specialist fostering service but is closely linked with the respite care scheme. Its history is interesting – started as a joint health/social services project aimed at getting children with learning difficulties out of the long stay mental health institution. Families were recruited and the placements were made under NHS legislation. Because of the basis of the scheme, there has always been a strong involvement of parents working alongside the professionals.

Only linked with fostering services in the last three years and it is now acknowledged as a specialist fostering scheme with quite a high profile. The service is available for children with a:
- severe learning disability
- physical disability
- sensory impairment
- degenerative disorder
- terminal illness

or any combination of these.

All long-term placements have built in respite. There are 29 placements currently of which nine are shared care. Carers meet bimonthly for mutual support and further training, and receive a fee plus a fostering allowance plus relevant state benefits.

3 May 95 I want to explore the idea of focusing on shared care as a project because there is obviously a need which falls between respite and full-time fostering. Not currently offered within the Department and fits well into Children Act philosophy. Maybe need to go back to Leeds and discuss in more detail and meet some carers/parents.

23 August 95 Meeting with Maureen, social worker with children's disability team, to talk about Rosie, a 10-year-old girl who has Rett Syndrome – profound physical disabilities and gradually losing what abilities she has. Living at home full time with her family but this will become less and less viable as she gets bigger. There's a time factor because her older sister, who is one of the main supports and does a lot of the physical caring, is leaving home to go to University next October, so Maureen is working on finding shared care by then.

Every parent, child and substitute family, whatever its function, should be given a placement package every time a new child is placed. Placement packages should not only include summaries of all available information, but guidance about access to information in the future. Appendix A is an example of information packages for the parents involved in adoption.

Honesty and trust

When prospective carers approach a family placement agency, they are expected to be honest and to entrust details of their lives to strangers. In return, they have a right to expect to be trusted with the truth at all times; the truth about a child and his/her disability, the truth about problems when they arise, and the truth about their application should they get turned down. If problems are not acknowledged and discussed along the way, families will justifiably be resentful if things go wrong. 'Why didn't you warn me?' asked a single man accusingly, when he was told at the end of an assessment that his housing situation was inadequate.

Case or line managers, assistant directors, the members of a panel and secretaries will probably all have access to information about the family. Unless confidentiality is defined to mean "confidential to the team", applicants could be led to believe that the interviewing social worker alone will know their story. Similarly, it needs to be said that sensitive information about a child's parents has to be restricted to the team, unless the child's safety or future well-being are at stake.

However democratic and open the assessment process is, the final responsibility for placing a child rests with the parents or guardian, or with a fostering/adoption panel, or with some other representative of the local authority. Self-assessment promises to produce a better assessment, but it cannot lead to self-approval. This has to be made plain at the very beginning. It is tempting to be vague because otherwise it could feel like giving self-determination with one hand and taking it away with the other. But families will work better if they know

exactly what they are doing and why they are doing it. We must surely believe that everyone wants to get it right for themselves as well as for the child. Attendance at panel would seem to be a reasonable expectation after all that hard work.

A service they can use and understand

Can parents who come to the agency to talk about a child, or families who come in response to a recruitment drive, understand English well enough to follow the aims and procedures of the organisation? Sometimes people give an appearance of understanding when they do not, because although they speak English fluently, the customs and formalities may be alien to their way of life. Might an interpreter, or another member of their community help? And is information available in locally used languages other then English?

Is jargon banned from all written material and avoided in meetings and workshops and during interviews – especially medical jargon about disability? Are forms simple and few?

Is the service anti-racist, anti-sexist, anti-ageist and anti-disablist in a practical sense? As disability is a central issue, is there wheelchair access, and are disabled applicants made comfortable?

Is the telephone answered promptly and is the caller transferred quickly to a named social worker who can deal with the matter? It is tiresome to leave messages for people who are in meetings or out of the office; better to indicate clearly the times and days when someone will be available, however limiting that may be.

Do families always know what to expect next? Are they consulted about times convenient for meetings and home visits and are the placement workers punctual? One of the main complaints of foster carers is that appointments are frequently changed at short notice and that social workers arrive late without consideration for family activities.

Discussed family placement and possible timescales for the idea of a shared care scheme. It would be too late for Rosie, if we wait until I do a feasibility study, work out more details, present to the Steering Group, get agreement to funding of placements and worker, etc. I'm beginning to wonder about simply looking for this resource for Rosie (and maybe Peter) and using it as a small pilot project. Needs further discussion and thought. Said I would get back to Maureen and let her know.

25 August 95 Really want to get going on trying to find shared care placements for Rosie and Peter. Will write a brief proposal and see what managers think.

4 September 95 Have formulated initial proposal on piloting shared care – reckon we'd have to pay a full fee all the time although the fostering allowances would be pro rata. Had a very useful second visit to Leeds scheme and met a number of carers.

NB. The state benefits eg Disability Living Allowance are still paid to the parents in the shared care placements so an agreement has to be reached between parents and carers.

I was struck by the ability of the shared care families to continue to see the children as belonging with their birth family. One family, which has developed a special feeling for children with autism, has been caring for an eight-year-old boy for many months on a full-time basis. He will probably remain with them for many more months if not years. Despite this, his identity is firmly rooted in his birth family, who are much valued by the shared carers. They see themselves clearly as caring for him on behalf of his parents who had reached the end of their tether in coping with his bizarre and disturbing behaviour. The carers' own need to be parents has been fully met by rearing their own children.

19 September 95 Firmed up the shared care proposal and discussed with Richard and Mike (managers in Disability Division). Both seemed enthusiastic. Mike will do some exploratory work re: funding.

Proposal for piloting a shared care scheme

I would like to propose that I use the opportunity of the two referrals I have had requesting shared care to pilot the idea of a shared care scheme. Since my post is for a limited period, it would be a good use of the time to establish whether shared care is a viable resource to develop. We do not offer any form of shared care at the moment. Respite care is limited to a maximum of 90 days per year and is usually much less. Shared care would offer significantly more alternative care for a child with disabilities in a substitute family – something we are not able to provide within fostering services because as soon as a child leaves a foster home it becomes available for another child.

The outcome of this small pilot scheme would give us information on which to base future decisions about the provision of share care. I propose the following process:

– Draw up pen pictures of the children in consultation, with the workers and families.
– Use these as the basis for any publicity.
– I suggest we pay a maximum fee to each family on a full time basis, and then pay the fostering allowance pro rata.
– I will manage the process of the publicity, response, assessment and approval of any family in close conjunction with the workers for the children.
– Support to any family we recruit would be given jointly by myself and the child's worker – if a full scheme is not developed, the children's workers would continue to support placements.

26 September 95 Agreement from managers to pilot the shared care scheme and proceed with recruitment for Rosie and Peter.

2 October 95 Have arranged visits to both Peter's family and Rosie's family to draw up the publicity material for children as accurately as possible, but concisely and in a lively, readable way.

Is the service sufficiently flexible to accommodate the pace at which people work best?

Two couples responded to publicity regarding two eight-year-old girls with learning difficulties who needed regular respite care. Both couples were equally keen to proceed; one family went from one stage to the next without a pause, while the other family took time to reflect and asked for more discussion with the child's worker and parents at each stage. The first family was ready three months before the second; in the end, each provided good care for one of the children. To delay the first family or to hurry the second could have lost either or both.

Is the service adaptable enough to recognise that all people do not learn in the same way? Some like to see everything in print and take copious notes, others do not like to read or write. Some are illiterate or have low literacy levels – could information be available on audiotape? Some learn in groups, others are immobilised by groups; some feel most receptive in their own homes, while others prefer neutral ground. It is usually not a good idea to make any particular procedure obligatory unless it is a statutory requirement.

How welcoming is the agency? Do families feel they are going to be "weeded out?" or "counselled in"?

How welcoming is the agency office? Does it look like a place where people are taken care of or does it resemble an anonymous institutional waiting room? Are tea and coffee available, maybe even with a biscuit?

References

1. Howe D, *Attachment Theory for Social Work Practice*, Macmillan, 1995.
2. *Be My Parent*, Bimonthly newspaper, BAAF. Also, *Focus on Fives*, fortnightly newsletter, BAAF.
3. *Adoption UK*, quarterly newsletter, PPIAS.

Dear Carer

- Are you looking for a new challenge?
- Do you have experience of, or a special interest in, caring for children with disabilities?
- Do you want to work from home?

If you answer YES or MAYBE to these three questions, you might be just who we're looking for to offer SHARED CARE to either Rosie or Peter.

Rosie is 10 years old, sociable, affectionate and totally physically dependent because she has Rett Syndrome. She loves bouncing on the bed, music, Disney videos, being with her sisters, and eating!

Peter is 12 years old, affectionate, fun to be with and can be stubborn. He has Down's Syndrome and can walk (slowly) and say a few words. He enjoys music, rough and tumble, and playing hide and seek.

As a shared carer, you will:

- Receive a fee of £118 per week plus a maintenance allowance.
- Work in partnership with the family.
- Work as part of a team.

Interested? Want to know more?

Come to an open Information Meeting.

Thursday 4th January 1996

T.F Davies Centre, Clifton Villas.
or telephone Ailie Kerrane ON 754325

Having got the go ahead to pilot the shared care scheme on a very small scale, I set about trying to recruit specific families for these two children.

Target group

In discussion with both workers, we agreed to target approved respite and foster carers initially. With hindsight, I would not have restricted the first trawl to approved carers.

Publicity

The process of devising publicity was very rewarding for me. It was exciting to work so closely with parents. As an Adoption and Fostering worker I have often produced pen-pictures of children for recruitment purposes, but never involved parents so directly.

When I visited Peter's mother to work on the wording for publicity, she had a very full and detailed report ready and waiting. I was delighted and surprised, because I knew she had difficulties with reading and writing, but she had found help and gave an excellent description of Peter. I only added a couple of anecdotes which came up in the conversation; they helped to lighten the text and bring it to life – otherwise it is entirely the mother's work.

Rosie's family was similarly involved in publicity and we sent out a leaflet to the 800 target households in December 1995.

Rosie is 10 years old

She is fun to be with, likes lots of activity going on around her, not a child for "just sitting pretty in her wheelchair". She's very sociable and has an infectious chuckle. Her personality and warmth shine through, despite major physical difficulties caused by Rett Syndrome which means she is totally physically dependent.

If you meet Rosie, you'll probably find her delightful, but it won't stop you being exhausted at the end of the day – she's heavy to lift, and although her house is adapted (including hoists and a lift), strong backs are still essential.

Flexibility is the key in what we're looking for for Rosie because she is constantly changing and so are the needs of her family, for example, her big sister goes off to college next year. We need a family with two carers who can share the care with Rosie's family, initially offering about one long weekend a month, probably increasing with time to equal sharing.

She lives in Newton and goes to school in Blackwood so carers within travelling distance would be essential.

Peter is 12 years old

He is affectionate, lovable, strong-willed (can be stubborn!) and is fun to be with. He likes playing ball, rough and tumble, playing hide and seek, bouncing (strong mattress required!), music, dancing and gardening. He loves to be outdoors but has only learned to walk recently. He likes animals (except horses) but they have to be long-suffering because Peter's way of playing with the cat can be a bit rough.

Peter has Down's Syndrome which has caused him to be quite slow at learning – he communicates mostly in signs and by touch and can say a few words like "Mum" and "no". He's learning to use the toilet but still needs a nappy at the moment. He needs help with washing and dressing.

He's a big strong lad and can sometimes squeeze or pinch people and hurt them without realising it. He's very trusting and therefore needs to be with an adult when he's out. Peter can't go out on his own and needs constant supervision at home too – just like a much younger child. His mum says caring for him can be exhausting, so it's lucky that he sleeps like a log all night.

We're looking for a carer who can look after Peter in their own home for about half of each week, sharing the care with his mother, who looks after him for the other half.

Training, preparation, introductions and support

Training

Anyone who is going to start a new job has a right to be trained or to be given the tools to train themselves. The purpose of training in substitute family care must be to assess the nature of the job and how it is to be done, and to enable families to assess whether to go on or to withdraw. There is no national curriculum, no end of course test and no diploma. The content, length, methods and number of participants will depend on the type of family care and the agency's resources.

Training should not only involve the principal carers, but also the other children in the family and relatives who might offer support, especially grandparents. There is no prescription for how or when to involve them; much will depend on age, availability and interest. After a recent introductory seminar for prospective adopters, there was a request to repeat the course for grandparents. The children of the family and any other members of the household should be included at every stage of the training and preparation process, but not in every session. Children should be encouraged to participate but should not be allowed to feel responsible for the decision to take a child with disabilities.

Training can be conveniently split into two parts: an introduction to relevant subject areas and an exploration of the family's needs and capabilities. The first part should cover child care and development, disability issues, attachment and separation, the demands and rewards of substitute family care, disability rights and benefits, the significance of gender, ethnicity, religion and culture, and general contact issues. These themes can be most satisfactorily discussed in groups as Part I – as long as groups are not put up as hurdles for people who cannot jump.

Prospective carers tell us that they learn most from people who are doing the job already. Adopters, foster carers and respite carers can make the best co-trainers or speakers. Some agencies "twin" carers in training with experienced carers of disabled children, to provide a much appreciated, informal back-up service. Groups also want to hear about disability from paediatricians, about special education from teachers, and about sexual abuse and behavioural problems from psychologists who have worked with disabled children.

Some groups enjoy exercises, others do not, but most are willing to share experiences. What people remember as most important about their own families of origin, how they separated from them, their first contact with disability, and their knowledge of children in need, will form a basis for joint work.

Group exercise

One of the most popular ways to learn about human growth and development, related to disability, is for each member of the group to be given a number of slips of paper with a description of a particular behaviour, like 'cries when left alone in the room'.

On a table are empty boxes labelled for ages 0-1, 2-4, 5-7, and so on. Everyone puts their slips in the boxes they consider appropriate for the behaviour described. The slips are then taken from each box in turn, read out and discussed. If the slip 'cries when left alone in the room' has been put in the 0-1 box, as would be reasonable, it creates an opportunity to compare normal development with that of an insecure child of ten who has learning difficulties and might react like a toddler.

The second part of the training has to do with each family's personal exploration of their own needs and capacities. I believe that it is impossible to assess someone's ability to do a job until they are doing it. I also know that anyone can con me if I set them up to prove themselves. 'Ask a silly question, get a silly answer' we used to say when we were little. I have learned to avoid questions and instead, to devise and invent tools, together with families, in order to discover their strengths and their weaknesses in a joint adventure.

The following are some ideas which have worked; families have found them helpful and the children in the families have given them top marks. The creative part of all the exercises is the thinking and discussion they provoke.

The 24 hour clock

Families draw a large clock on a sheet of card and divide it into 24 sections. They fill in how they normally spend a day and night. Then they add what they think a disabled child coming into the family will be doing. Is there enough space in the day for the child? And how do they feel about broken nights?

Before and after

How do families see themselves now and how do they think others see them? How do they imagine they will be seen with a disabled child? How will they deal with ignorant comments?

A young family with three children born to them adopted Harry, a four-year-old boy with Down's Syndrome. He fitted in neatly between the one-year-old toddler and a girl of six. The oldest daughter, aged ten, was particularly attached to Harry, and became deeply upset when she overheard a woman in a supermarket say: 'They ought to be strangled at birth when they're like that.'

19 December 95 I'm optimistic about the response to the shared care flyer. A dozen phone calls so far. About half and half foster and respite carers. Most of the foster carers wanted to know if having younger children placed with them would rule them out. I encouraged them to come to the meeting while explaining that ideally Peter would do better where he was the youngest.

4 January 96 Having had 12 phone calls I was hopeful of a good turn out for the Information Meeting. It was disappointing – only three households came. One of those looked very promising for Peter – a woman already working on the respite care scheme who came with her teenage son.

One couple – experienced foster carers – were interested in Rosie.

8 January 96 Telephoned the other families who had responded to the flyer. Most people had decided against, but I made arrangements to visit two of the families to have more discussion.

January/February 96 Visits to the two families who did not attend the Information Meeting and to the three families who did. The two foster families who had not attended were both interested in shared care in principle but were not suitable for either of the two children. One couple was already caring for a profoundly disabled, very dependent child who would not be compatible with either Peter or Rosie. The other was a single foster carer who had two very active pre-school children placed at the moment. Both these families would like to be kept informed.

Of the three who attended, one is looking very promising for Peter – I will discuss both families who were interested in Peter with Bob (his social worker). The foster carers who expressed an interest in Rosie are coming to the end of a difficult placement and will need a break. Also they're not ideal geographically. We'll have to wait and see. Unfortunately no other possibilities for Rosie.

28 March 96 I am faced with a variety of different tasks for these two children:
PETER – having identified a family, the work now is to prepare, assess, and hopefully approve them as foster carers for Peter.

And what about comments from people who are not supposed to be ignorant?

> *The same family took Harry to the doctor with a persistent cough. The doctor barely glanced at Harry before he said, 'You have to remember he's a Down's Syndrome child'.*

Rules

People are asked to write down all the rules in the family in three columns: rules that are unimportant in the first column; rules that matter but may be broken in the second column; and rules that may not be broken in the third column. If it is a couple, do both agree on the categories? Can they contemplate living with a child who may not comprehend any rules at all? How would they help a child to learn the rules that must be obeyed for the sake of harmony, fairness and safety? Some families at first insist that there are no rules in their household. But as soon as they remember that the children can't help themselves to sweets, or that they mustn't flush the toilet at night, or have to brush their feet when they come in from the garden, the three columns begin to fill up.

Questionnaires

This works only for couples. Both are asked to fill in the same questionnaire separately without talking about it together. The questionnaire can be adapted to fit different situations but is basically made up of a series of questions about who does what in the house, how family holidays and outings are organised, who takes big decisions and who takes small decisions, and who pays the bills. How much does it cost to provide a meal, buy a pair of shoes, have a haircut, and then go swimming with a seven-year-old child? The interest lies not in the answers, which are in any case not intended for the worker, but in the inevitable discrepancies of perception, when the couple compares notes. Apparently many prospective male carers think that a pair of shoes for a seven-year-old can still be bought for a fiver, whereas some women are unaware that they discourage their partner from taking an interest in such things. Couples usually

feed back that the exercise helps them to understand how they function and how they might be seen by others. It also enables them to consider how each of them might manage if they stopped being a couple. This is more relevant to child care today than trying to forecast the durability of a marriage or any other relationship.

Lists

It is often useful to draw up lists. It jogs the memory, makes us feel we are in control, and helps us to concentrate on a task. Lists of all the challenging, irritating, disturbing, distressing and provoking behaviours a child could exhibit are then sorted out into what would be acceptable, tolerable and beyond bearing. Plenty of scope for further discussion there. It is surprising how many people are more horrified by greed than by deliberate vomiting. Do most of us have to work so hard to control our own greed that we cannot forgive an uninhibited approach to food, material possessions, and above all, to love? Other lists can be drawn up: lists of what the family has to offer others and what the family needs, lists of family members who would be involved or just interested in the placement, leading to exploration of the importance of contact and continuity; lists of family rituals and traditions to which any child would have to be introduced; or lists of barriers and problems a family might have to face, for instance, a lone parent or a gay couple. Clearly, there is no limit to how lists can be made to fit individual circumstances, or to how exercises can be devised to cover each family's agreed training programme.

Preparation

In addition to training, there has to be preparation for a particular child if it is to be permanent care, or for a specific service if it is to be short-term care. It is self-evident that all of the training as well as the preparation must have clearly stated aims, so that the one can follow and build on the other in a meaningful way. Most families like to have a written programme covering the combined content of their preparation and training; they want to know what they will be doing and why.

Exchanging life stories

This is the time for families to learn more about the child they are hoping to have, or the kind of children they may care for in the future. The child's history must now be presented in detail, so that needs, including contact needs, can be examined in the light of what the family has to offer. Just as children will come with life story books, so families should make their own, on audio/video cassettes, in writing, and with photographs to introduce themselves. It is a good way to concentrate on the child's understanding – to imagine home and family as the child will see them and to find a way of showing that there is a place for her or him or them.

> *Sheilagh and Ben, who fostered several children with a variety of disabilities, drew a family tree for each child in turn. It was a drawing of a real tree, not a diagram, and it had a branch for every member of the growing family, with a photograph hanging from it. Every time a new child was introduced, the tree grew a new branch with an empty photograph frame which said "Waiting for Johnny" or Mary or whoever it was going to be.*

After families have produced a children's version of their story, they can go on to start work on a profile of themselves for the panel or other decision-making body. Some couples prefer to write each other's histories rather than their own. And why not?

Family systems and contact

Each family not only has its own story to tell, it also has its own set of values, beliefs, customs – its way of dealing with the world and of interpreting the world. Every family works according to its own system and develops its own myths. When a new child joins the family, two family systems meet.

ROSIE – *having found no one in this first attempt, we need to plan and work on the next step, or give up the search. If we do continue, the recruitment must have a geographical focus. Rosie is familiar with her local school and hospital and they know her very well. So there is little point in considering any national publicity – we must contact local papers, schools, libraries, clinics, and hospitals and involve her parents in ideas about target groups.*

So we go back to the recruitment process for Rosie while moving on to the next stages with Peter. What started out as a joint project is now dividing into separate pieces of work.

A similar balancing act has developed for the twins, Andrew and Gary. A review decision, based on an assessment done by the respite unit, was made to separate the boys and see if that would make family placements more feasible – the foster carers who looked after them had always maintained they would be manageable separately but their different needs made it impossible to care for them together. While we were deciding how to proceed with family-finding, a couple came forward for Andrew. Both work within the field of disability, know the twins slightly, and when they heard that separate placements were being sought, felt they could meet Andrew's needs. The process of working with them towards a placement has now begun. But, as yet, there is no similar offer for Gary. So now we have the problem of:
– working with one potential family towards approval as foster carers for Andrew;
– trying to recruit a family for Gary, targeting publicity towards people working in special schools, disability units;
– trying to plan/adjust the timescales of the two tasks so that the boys can move together.

Barriers to placement

BEFORE *moving on to look at the next stage of the placement process, there is an important point to make about attitude and belief in the possibility of finding placements. This is summed up by a quotation from Against the Odds by Catherine Macaskill:*[1]

'Staff attitude was sort of neutral veering towards dislike, and none of the staff said they wanted to work on such placements. It is impossible to estimate how much public interest is lost through this approach... enthusiasm and commitment were the exception. But, for those who have placed mentally handicapped children... experience has always led to interest.'

Each family will have its own attitudes to violence, discipline, sex, alcohol, drugs, sickness, honesty, "race", religion, politics, charity, education, work, money, social workers, and of course, disability. Can they fit comfortably together? Continuity and contact are the most common areas of conflict and misunderstanding if they do not. There is an obvious parallel here to marriage and seeing the in-laws. How does each family value the generations? How do the family members keep in touch and what do they mean by keeping in touch – a telephone call at Christmas, an occasional letter, formal visits by arrangement or popping in and out of each other's homes? Is the telephone a usual means of communication or do they write letters? Do they give frugally or extravagantly for birthdays – and who considers what is extravagant, and why? What is appropriate behaviour when you meet? Do you hug, kiss, cuddle, shake hands or keep your distance? Do you tell all to each other or do you wait to be asked and then give nothing away? Do you dress up or dress down for a visit? Is the room too hot or too cold, too bare or too grand? Does punctuality matter? How do distance, methods of transport, travel sickness and income influence each family's view of contact?

At this point in the preparation process, it is essential to make families aware of their own family system and of the particular system a child will come from. Contact and continuity plans can then be made based on understanding and tolerance, especially if the child has been abused, neglected or rejected. It is never safe to leave these arrangements until later.

Contact with birth families is as important an issue for disabled children as for all children who have to be separated from their parents. It is never good enough to presume that a child does not comprehend the meaning of relationships and that therefore contact is insignificant. On the contrary, it could be argued that only if contact with the family of origin is maintained, can a child with learning difficulties make sense of her world, or a child with physical disabilities accept himself as he is.[1]

Families should believe that contact, if it is at all possible, will enhance a placement; they should not be asked to agree to contact as a condition or as an inducement.

Expert advice and guidance

Everyone who has been involved with the child will have something to add to the family's preparation. Parents have the most significant contribution to make, but teachers, previous carers, educational psychologists, health visitors, residential workers, paediatricians, psychiatrists and specialists in disability could all give invaluable expert advice and answer questions that have arisen. There is a danger, however, of swamping families with too many opinions, so we must be careful to "dance half a step behind" – a memorable metaphor used by my first social work tutor to point out that it is not up to us to set the pace. The agency medical adviser can be a source of help and guidance and should be able to collate and interpret medical reports to make them more digestible.

If children have been sexually abused, families will need to know how to deal with sexualised behaviour, how to set clear sexual boundaries, how to protect other children and how to handle disclosures and painful memories. Abuse of disabled children is hard to contemplate; expert help should be made available to prepare a family for an abused child but it will not always be known if children have been abused, especially if they have communication problems. And it should never be assumed that any child is too disabled to be sexually abused.[2] The level of intimate care many disabled children require puts them at greater risk in every setting.

Finding out

The best way to learn is to find out for yourself. Families who are going to look after a child, or several children with disabilities, need to know about their local resources and services. It is a task during the preparation period, which most families enjoy as a relief from all the serious thinking and assessing they are embroiled in. They go and look at schools, speak to the head-teachers about further education, talk to their GP about taking on a disabled child, explore the day care and employment opportunities for disabled school-leavers in their area, and obtain details of services and support groups for all disabled children – at their own pace, of course!

If they have not had any previous experience of looking after disabled children, prospective carers should have the opportunity "to practise". Most organisations are pleased to have a few extra pairs of hands for an outing, and families who already care for disabled children can provide the most tangible introduction to disability, especially for the younger members of the family-in-waiting.

If aids and appliances are going to be needed for a particular child, then it is as well to get familiar with them before the child moves in.

> *Leslie was a fourteen-year-old with brittle bone disease who used a wheelchair. He was placed with short-term foster carers while his grandmother, who was also his guardian, had to go into hospital. Leslie was well prepared for the move and the carers had fostered other children with disabilities. But they had never accommodated a wheelchair. They found Leslie delightful and the wheelchair impossible. They had a good piece of advice for the social worker: 'If you want to find a home for a child in a wheelchair, place the wheelchair first, and when it's settled, introduce the child.'*

Claiming and independence

By this time, families should be ready to work out how they will claim this child they have prepared for. "Claiming" has become a useful word to describe any activity which makes children feel that they belong and that it is safe to become attached. The degree of claiming desirable will depend upon the kind of care being offered. Just as relatives or friends do not lay the same claim on a child as parents do, so it would be quite wrong for respite carers to attempt to claim a child as completely as permanent carers must. 'But isn't it all instinctive?' people ask. Well, yes, it is for some, but it never does any harm to be prepared to help claiming along.

And one of her conclusions from that study:

'Professional attitudes towards mentally handicapped children, and towards the type of families who volunteered for their adoption, are major barriers to the progress of this work... The common bond uniting most professionals was a predominantly negative attitude to mental handicap.'

This study was of adoption agencies; the professionals referred to are adoption and fostering specialists.

In working on the case of Andrew and Gary, I have been struck by the impact of such attitudes, including my own. These twins had developed a "reputation" within the Adoption and Fostering Unit, and were seen as exceptionally difficult to place. This was, of course, reinforced when their placement with very experienced carers broke down and they had to move to a residential unit. There is no doubt that they are difficult to care for, and that therefore it would be hard to find them a family. Moreover, because the belief in family placement as a real possibility had gone, the advice I gave was to abandon the search and look for a long-term residential alternative.

However, when a family came forward for Andrew, we decided once more to pursue family placement for both boys. We then had a meeting with the head of the residential respite unit where the boys live and the combination of his optimism and enthusiasm, with the reality of a potential family for one of them, helped to inject us with the energy we needed to look for another family.

The head of the home's perspective on the boys was radically different from mine. He did not see them as seriously disabled or particularly difficult to care for individually – within his context they were the most able children, although most disruptive when together. He felt acutely that they were inappropriately placed in his unit, and was convinced that there must be people "out there" who could successfully parent them. He and his staff have created a pen picture of Gary and have identified a useful target group for recruitment. This group includes all staff working in special schools and disability units (both adult and children's) as well as informal networks, to get the message across that we are looking for foster families for disabled children. We don't know whether we'll find a family, but there's certainly a hundred per cent greater chance now that we're actively looking and have a sense of optimism.

There are endless opportunities for claiming during every ordinary day: a pet name, a new toothbrush like mine, a story about how we first saw you, a magic flower from the garden to make a wish, something to collect together – leaves, or stones, or transfers, or anything, baking a cake, having an adventure on the way back from the shops, sharing a joke or a secret, taking photographs of the family, visiting gran who makes the best chocolate biscuits or uncle Harry who has the biggest ears, allotting a special household task like polishing the mirror or helping to care for a pet, and devising a bedtime ritual which reassures and leaves a light on.

Families become impressively inventive once they get the idea; and the idea is to give quality attention. Not the kind of attention most of us give while we peel the potatoes, plan the next day's travel arrangements, watch the television or listen to the other children squabbling upstairs, but truly undivided attention. Life has to go on, and the potatoes do have to be peeled as well as all the other things that happen in families, and no-one would suggest that any child should or could have undivided attention all the time. However, I was taught by a family which fostered and successfully "claimed" three blind children, that even fifteen minutes of real attention is better than any amount of listening or playing or looking after with half a mind. This family used massage as a way of paying attention – foot massage that was unintrusive but established physical contact with older children who did not trust being touched.

Children who have been claimed must in due course separate and become independent. It is difficult to prepare for adulthood before a child has even joined a family, especially if the child is disabled to a degree that will not allow him or her to be independent in the accepted sense. But that makes it more urgent to plan ahead and consider what level of independence will be possible and how this could be achieved. Attachment and separation are on opposite sides of the same coin. Separation need not necessarily mean a physical departure, but even the most disabled young people can and should be allowed to become adults.

Support

Families who undertake training and preparation to look after other people's children have a right to expect our support; support to carry on and support to withdraw. If families feel supported in their efforts rather than tested, they will be able to withdraw without a sense of failure. It is only when we present them with an obstacle race of forms and conditions and criteria that they will make an unreasonable dash for the winning post.

Families also need material support. Enhanced foster care allowances, adoption allowances, generous retainers for short-term and respite carers and payments for special needs, including contact arrangements, should be readily available. As we know that it is three times more expensive to bring up children with disabilities than other children, it is not logical to approve families to do a job and then prevent them from doing it properly.

Respite care should be built in as a support system for all long-term carers. Often new families cannot believe that they will ever want to make use of it – never mind, as long as they know it is there for them, they can take a raincheck on it.

Catherine, a single woman, adopted Shirley, a little girl with Diabetes Insipidus and impaired vision who required almost constant attention. Catherine gave up her work in a hospital so that she could look after Shirley full time. She had looked after several disabled children in the hospital and could not imagine that she would need help with only one child in her own home and nothing to distract her. She did indeed manage for eighteen months without a break; then Shirley had a spell of illness and Catherine was up day and night for a week. When Shirley recovered, Catherine was exhausted. She found the piece of paper with the details of the local respite care scheme and used it. She went on using it after that to prevent further exhaustion. She said that she could not have brought herself to ask for respite care if her right to have it had not been made explicit from the beginning.

Preparation and assessment

8 December 95 Phone call from Jackie – she had just received the description of Peter along with the respite carers' newsletter. She is a respite carer for a profoundly deaf six-year-old boy. She was enthusiastic and excited on the phone – very keen, something she'd been hoping to do for years and Peter sounded just right.

4 January 96 Jackie, a single parent, and her 15-year-old son, Ian, came to the Information Meeting and both were obviously involved, enthusiastic and committed.

Jackie and Ian waited patiently while Peter's social worker and I made contact with everyone who had expressed an interest in Peter, until we finally selected them as the family most likely to meet Peter's needs. There had been one other respite carer (who had also attended the information meeting) and had been interested in Peter. So it was really a choice between the two respite carers. After visiting the other carer, I felt she did not have the energy, commitment or patience required to care for Peter.

11 March 96 Visited Jackie and Ian to begin the assessment/preparation process. They have already been waiting three months, with little happening from their point of view. Used this first visit to get to know them and explain the process and how long it might take. I also looked round the house. Was disappointed to find they only have two bedrooms which could prove problematic. Ian is willing to share but I think this needs further thought. Peter is not used to sharing his bedroom at home and Ian may want to preserve his own space and privacy as he gets older. I still feel very positive about this application and am sure we can get round the practical problems given the amount of enthusiasm and commitment around.

Having managed adoption and fostering services for many years, this opportunity to be closer to the applicant's perspective is a very useful, if salutary, experience for me. It has made me reconsider some of the long held tenets of preparation work. For example, in our unit, each applicant must attend a series of preparation meetings prior to being allocated a worker for the individual assessment. This is based on the belief that there is a body of knowledge and understanding essential for any carer. The first stage gives them an opportunity to learn more, and then opt out if they wish. The idea has merit, but in a large organisation, dealing with many applicants for different schemes and types of caring, an unlucky applicant could wait months for the relevant preparation group.

In my own work with Jackie and Ian, it will be different because it is a new pilot scheme and focused on a particular child. So the delay will be shorter, the individual assessment and preparation will begin immediately, and hopefully we can fit in a preparation group at some other stage.

18 March 96 Visited Jackie and Ian. We concentrated on the day to day aspects of their lives, and how this might be affected by Peter joining their family. Ian was there for most of the interview and we used diagrams to illustrate their interest, who is important to them, and what problems they have dealt with together.

25 March 96 Supervision session. Discussed protection of disabled children from abuse, particularly in a family placement.

We must build in extra protection for disabled children, because of their increased vulnerability – how can we do this within a family placement setting? In a residential unit, procedures can ensure that potentially abusive situations are reduced to a minimum, although even here it can be difficult to implement, and at times impossible with cut budgets and consequent lower staffing levels.

Other forms of support like a home help, childminding one evening a week, relief in the holidays, transport facilities, nurseries and youth clubs should be on offer, although not necessarily all of them for every family. It can be hard to find even a babysitter for a small child with severe epilepsy, as Jane and Michael discovered when they adopted Rosie.

To begin with, Jane and Michael didn't want to leave Rosie with anyone else, but when they felt more confident about controlling her fits, no-one they knew was willing to take responsibility for a whole evening. They didn't want to go back to the agency because nothing had been said about practical post-placement support and they were worried about being seen as failures. So they just stopped going out together until a researcher picked up what was happening and supported an application to social services for a trained babysitter.

In some other areas, a babysitter might have been found from among members of MENCAP or one of the organisations listed at the end of this book, but new families of children with disabilities need encouragement to join such organisations. Substitute carers are not always made welcome by birth parents and the ground may have to be prepared for them. After all, it is understandable that families who did not choose to have a disabled child should be wary of those who do. When alternative carers do join disability associations, it is often a mutually rewarding experience for all the families.

Support networks of friends and relations also have to be developed and nurtured. It may be presumed that grandparents, aunts, uncles, cousins and good friends, who have ever been helpful, will rally round if needed. But if they have not been taken along the preparation way, they could feel apprehensive about a disability they do not understand, and uncertain about what role they might play. Part of the support from the agency placing the children is to sort out how the family, especially single carers, will be supported by others.

Planned introductions

When substitute carers have finally been approved and children are waiting, there is still further work ahead before a placement can happen, introductions will have to be precisely planned to be right for the child and right for the family. What is right will depend on the age of the child, the disability, the kind of placement, the distances to be covered, the time available and the growth of trust and confidence.

A precise plan is not a rigid plan; it must allow for rapid as well as slow progress. And it must be closely monitored in order to be responsive to unforseeable circumstances and unpredictable reactions. The details of the plan should be agreed in advance with everyone concerned: parents, present carers, new family, social workers, and if at all possible, with the child. How will the first meeting be managed and where and when will it take place? Who will be present, how long will it last, and who will bring the child and take the child back? Will the child's birth family be involved in introductions, and if so, how? What means can be found to help a disabled child get to know new people and a strange environment? Who will be responsible for collecting feed back after each visit, keeping everyone informed and co-ordinating each stage of the plan? How will the family keep in touch with the child between meetings – with postcards, phone calls or by some other means? How frequent should meetings be and how long should introductions take? It can safely be said that all introductions are as long as the proverbial piece of string and that every introduction plan will be unique.

Some families are extremely creative; the family which fostered three blind children introduced themselves and their home through touch and smell and sound. They always wore the same clothes, tie, necklace, perfume and after shave, and the same shoes with clicking heels. They played the same music on a portable cassette player and they gave a copy of the cassette to the children to keep between visits.

The first child had to make the move from hospital to family. Angela was a fearful four-year-old who had spent a large part of her life in treatment. She had a serious heart condition apart from her blindness, and needed skillful health care. There was no hope of contact with her birth parents. The foster family travelled a long distance every weekend for a month. They stayed at a hotel almost next door to the hospital and spent all their time with Angela until they were able to look after her on their own. Each time they visited they brought one of their grown up children to meet her. After a month, Angela seemed to be as ready to move as she would ever be. It was agreed that it would be confusing for her to be taken to visit her new home first; this was a child who had never been taken anywhere to visit and she would not have understood the reasons for coming and going.

For the second child, the programme was reversed. The family was no longer as mobile, and Andrew, aged six, was fiercely attached to a young residential worker in his small children's home. This worker had been instrumental in finding a family for Andrew, but she was dubious about this family taking on two blind children. So was his single mother, who had already met the carers. The residential worker took Andrew by car or train or bus twice a week to see the family in their home. On two occasions she also brought Andrew's mother. At first she stayed with him all the time, then increasingly she withdrew until Andrew was spending the day there while she went shopping in the nearest town. After four visits, the worker and Andrew went for the weekend; the worker stayed for one night, Andrew stayed for two. The foster carers took him back on Monday to the children's home and collected him the following Thursday for good. The residential worker came to visit the following Sunday.

This introduction plan served to encourage Andrew to trust and extend his attachments, and to reassure both the mother and the residential worker that the family could manage.

Within a family setting, we can introduce "safe caring" policies like same sex caring for intimate bodily tasks, and male members of the household not being alone with female children, but this can prove impossible to monitor effectively. We may have to accept the unpalatable fact that every care situation carries an element of risk. Our main tool in providing protection for any child is the building of trust and openness between the agency, carers and birth families, while still being vigilant about signs of abuse, and being clear about how we will investigate any concern.

26 March 96 *In planning this assessment I am rigorously asking what is the most effective and relevant way to prepare Jackie and Ian for sharing their lives with Peter? Peter's social worker and I decided to start with a meeting between the prospective carers and Peter and his mother at her house. We felt it was pointless proceeding if the initial building blocks were not there, and we were looking for answers to some basic questions: Is the chemistry right? Is Peter the kind of child they were expecting? Did Peter's mother feel she could work with Jackie? Could they all like each other enough?*

4 April 96 *Visited Jackie and Ian. We talked about sexuality and its expression in children, adolescents and adults. We explored the risk of sexual involvement between Ian and Peter and ways of reducing this risk. We also talked about the importance of "telling" if anything which seems wrong happens. Peter's mother has been involved in discussions about Peter's emerging sexuality and the issues it will present for any carer. Both Jackie and Ian seem very open about sexual matters, and grasped the potential risks inherent in the situation, including their own vulnerability. The presence of a maturing sexual being with the intellect and understanding of a much younger child can be a powerful trigger – either for experimentation, or unresolved issues being inappropriately acted out. I feel that the best protection we can give Peter is openness, understanding and trust, as well as working with him to enable him to know when things are wrong and how he can tell.*

While maintaining an optimistic view of humanity, it is important to know that systematic abusers may well target disabled children and find their way into a caring role. We must therefore have systems in place which try to screen out these potential abusers. As we know, this is not as easy as it sounds since abusers can often be "nice people" with apparently good understanding of children.

It also helped to make the family feel confirmed as capable carers and to lay the foundation of satisfactory contact arrangements. The mother, who was about to get married and had intended not to see Andrew again, now planned to introduce her husband to Andrew in the foster home and to maintain regular, though infrequent contact.

The third child, who had undiagnosed multiple disabilities and was still an infant, had been abandoned in hospital by parents who apparently left the country and could not be found. He had the briefest introduction. The whole family, which had by then acquired a wheelchair for Angela and a vehicle to hold all of them, motored a hundred miles to spend a day with the baby and took him back with them. There was simply no point in doing anything else for anyone's sake.

Post-placement services

When children are placed with substitute families, those families have a right to a post-placement service whether they offer long or short-term care, whether they foster or adopt. It is a statutory requirement under the Children Act 1989, the Adoption Act 1976, and the Adoption (Scotland) Act 1978 as amended by the Children (Scotland) Act 1995.

All children with disabilities have a right to services and children in substitute family care retain that right. Children who need extra care are not going to be easy to bring up. However thorough the training, preparation and introductions have been, the real work starts when the children are placed. Over and over again, people tell us that nothing and no-one could have told them what it was really going to be like.

The best post-placement service is simply a continuation of what has gone before. Families will still need information, a service they can understand, honesty and trust, expert advice, training and preparation for changing circumstances and different life stages, and

always support. This is not exactly the same as reviews twice a year and visits to check that all is well.

More information

- In the very first place, families must be able to rely on the placement agency to pass on all necessary information to schools, GPs, health visitors and relevant local authority departments. The agency medical adviser will usually take responsibility for transferring medical records.

- Families should be kept informed of any changes in the benefit system, income tax regulations and local authority allowances. Disability benefits are getting more complicated and there is no reason why people who make good carers should be able to fill in forms.

- They should also be informed of any changes in local authority policy or in the child's birth family and about any research or advances in treatments of specific conditions.

An ongoing useable service

Does the service suit? Does it fit in with the family's lifestyle, culture and religion? Does it take into account the child's disability and is it consistent? Does the agency provide a creche or other facilities to free carers to attend meetings? Is the family satisfied?

Consolidation of honesty and trust

Relatives, neighbours and friends may be too polite, too perplexed or too anxious to be perfectly frank about a placement; or they may simply be unaware of the progress and the problems which seem minor to the lay observer, but momentous to the family living through them. Carers have described placement workers as mirrors and sounding boards, providing a patient ear and a true reflection of what they see.

Yvette, who had adopted a quadriplegic teenager, talked almost non-stop the first Monday evening in the month, when the social worker called her on the telephone, by arrangement. She would always finish by saying, 'That was grand, now I've recharged my batteries'. Yvette also relied on the worker to tell her truly how she perceived the placement when she visited twice a year. The worker could feed back how much progress had been made, but she could also alert the adopter to any looming trouble spots.

Families have a right to know if social workers see warning signs – it is no good to say, when it is too late, that we saw it coming. On the other hand, families need to trust enough to be able to say themselves when something is not working. Even if there is no solution except disruption.

Expert advice and training by request

Carers of all kinds need the guidance of a variety of experts at different stages. Special education, sexual development of children with disabilities, medical conditions, behavioural problems and sexual abuse, are the subjects families most often want to learn more about. Study days, workshops or seminars for groups of carers are the most interesting and economical way of offering training with guest speakers. Unfortunately families prefer weekends while speakers and social workers do not, but weekends it may have to be. Some enterprising carers have organised their own residential weekend seminars; they ask the agency to pay for the speakers they themselves book, and then invite their social workers. It would be churlish to refuse such an invitation.

Further preparation

We all have to prepare for the life stages which change family systems: going to school, leaving school, births, marriages and deaths in the family, leaving home, separation and divorce, chronic sickness and unemployment or retirement.

In addition, while trying to "detect" abusers, we must also recognise that no system will be infallible; building alliances of adults working with vulnerable children will allow them to "blow the whistle" when abuse is suspected.

15 April 96 *We had the initial meeting between Julia – Peter's mother – and Jackie, which was very positive, last week and we are now planning the rest of the process. We have decided to keep up the momentum of the contact, and plan to have a second meeting at Jackie's house, so that Peter's mother can look round.*

22 April 96 *Peter and his mother, Julia, visited Jackie and Ian at their house. It went very well. The added bonus was that Julia commented on various aspects of safety and practical alterations which would be necessary in the house. These are not major adaptations, but will involve some planning and organisation.*

For a different child, like Rosie, practical implications regarding housing, and the physical strength of the carers, would be a major consideration.

24 April 96 *We will be building in some more contact, approximately one meeting per week between all the key participants, and continue to explore how the new family will need to adjust their lives to accommodate Peter. During this time Jackie and Ian will be storing up a bank of direct, relevant information about the reality of caring for Peter and negotiating with his mother. I anticipate this being the main basis of the preparation and assessment work. In addition, when talking to Jackie and Ian about their own backgrounds and life stories, I will be using my knowledge of the impact of a new child on any family system to help prepare them for a radical change in their lives.*

30 April 96 *Final assessment visit to Jackie and Ian to go over the BAAF Form F[2] and make any necessary alterations or additions. I have written it based on my discussions with them. They found the prospect of that amount of writing too daunting. They were both happy with what I had written and felt it reflected them accurately.*

Disability, like adoption, is a life factor and will influence the whole family's adaptation to change. Moreover, substitute family care involves the life stages of two families.

A sensitive response at the right time, which echoes earlier preparation and may include counselling other children in the family, can ease a sticky transition from one stage to the next and help to keep the placement intact.

Continuing support

- Children with disabilities attract many professionals. The local GP, a health visitor, a speech therapist, one worker for the deaf and another for the blind, an educational psychologist, specialist teachers and social workers may all be involved with the same family. They can give invaluable guidance, but they can leave families feeling overwhelmed, confused and invaded. A post-placement worker can effectively support the family by co-ordinating these services to make them more user friendly and to heighten awareness of foster care and adoption.

- Families with disabled children too often have to fight for their aids, adaptations, allowances and appliances, as well as for suitable housing and transport. Some families are better at fighting than others, but a little support from their social worker will rarely come amiss.

- Respite care for long-term carers may not work as smoothly as intended, or families may need support to give themselves permission to use it, however good it is. While asking for respite care should never be equated with failure, we do have to recognise a cry for help which is more than a request for temporary relief. Families need support to allow a placement to disrupt as well as to keep it going. They deserve respect for their feelings and recognition of their attempts to persevere. But if a placement cannot work, then at least with support, it can end in an orderly manner, so that it will do the least damage to child and family.

- If there is contact between a child and the birth family, it is likely that support will be required – not necessarily all the time, but both families must know that they will not be on their own if conflicts of interest arise. If the contact has to be supervised, carers must be quite clear about what is expected of them.

- A great deal of informal support can come from other carers but may require some back-up from the agency. Local shared interest groups or a telephone link service could become valued mutual support networks.

- One voluntary agency, in a metropolitan borough, invited the permanent foster carers and adopters with disabled children to join a telephone directory scheme. Information about each family was entered on separate pages in a loose leaf folder and included details about the disability, schools, playgroups or nurseries attended, medical and domiciliary services in use, and contact arrangements.

The Smith family rang up the Benistone family when their daughter was due to start school, because they saw in the directory that the Benistone's son, who had the same disability, went to a mainstream school in their neighbourhood. After some negotiations, and with the Benistone's help, their daughter was admitted to the same school.

Sarah discovered wonderful but expensive incontinence aids for her adopted teenage daughter. She put it down on her directory page and was inundated with enquiries. The families then got together and persuaded their local authorities to make a special allowance to foster families with incontinent older children.

It is often matters as mundane as disposable nappies or an efficient incontinence laundry service, which make a difficult placement run smoothly.

If we listen to families and hear what they say, it is likely that we will get it right for them, because once children are in placement, families know what they want and the questions they should ask. It is easier to read the map when you are standing on the spot marked "you are here". And if we follow half a step behind while we provide a post-placement service, we will learn more from them, our partners, about substitute family care for children with disabilities.

Finally, being a substitute family for children with disabilities is not all hard work. People who do it speak of the rewards more than of the problems. And like all families, they have fun. The high point of the year for one large group of foster carers and adopters is the annual picnic in congenial, spacious surroundings, where they spend the day chatting and playing with each other's children, comparing notes, exchanging tips and enjoying the stupendous amounts of food they bring to share with each other.

References

1 Argent H, *Post-adoption services for children with disabilities*, Practice paper published by the Post Adoption Centre, 1996.
2 Kennedy M, 'Children with Severe Disabilities: Too many assumptions' in *Child Abuse Review*, 1: 3, 1992.

We could be moving towards the full shared care arrangement as soon as the Form F and approval by the fostering panel are completed. If things do not go well, we shall be adjusting the level of contact accordingly and if, for some reason, the placement cannot proceed, we shall gradually reduce contact. Of course it is a risk to involve Peter from the beginning because he may have to be disappointed and hurt, but whenever we introduce a child to a new family we take that risk. Decisions about timing need to be carefully made, and we were influenced in this case by the fact that Jackie is already an approved respite carer, so that all the statutory checks had been done.

8 May 96 *I spent the morning completing the Form F on Jackie and Ian. So, it's almost exactly a year from when I first met with Peter's social worker – a year to recruit and prepare a shared care family and bring them to the point of approval. Not too bad – about average for a child of Peter's age and disability.*

References

1 Macaskill C, *Against the Odds*, BAAF, 1985
2 Form F, *Information on prospective substitute parents*, BAAF. This form has now been revised and is available as Form F1, *Information on prospective substitute parent(s)*, Form F2 *Information on prospective carer(s) for a specific known child*.
A new part III, *Additional information on physical disabilities/learning disabilities*, enables specific and relevant information to be collected on a child with disabilities.

SECTION **FOUR**

Residential care

A placement of choice?

'Unlike the parents of children in boarding schools who have chosen group living for their children, residential care has been seen by many social workers since the mid 1970s as a last resort when all else fails. Currently both national policy and good practice are focused on changing this prejudiced approach and moving towards recognising group care as an essential part of the spectrum of services for children.'[1]

In some other countries, residential or group care for children who cannot grow up with their own families is highly regarded as the preferred specialist option. Residential homes have been given a bad name in our system in the UK because they originated as institutions to give shelter rather than skilled care, and because we do not value communal living. Since the mid 1970s, there has been a major move to close children's homes, including special provision for disabled children, and what remains is often used by social workers guiltily and without any clear aim.

In contrast, parents of disabled children may expect a great deal from residential services if they believe that trained staff must be more expert than any family could be. Consequently, residential workers in group homes for disabled children can be left feeling both undermined and overburdened. There is surely a more positive way to view group care and a more purposeful way to organise it. If we want higher standards of residential services for disabled children, then we must treat the concept of group care with respect and learn to assess what it can offer the children for whom it will be appropriate.

Before residential care is pursued as the placement of choice for a specific child, certain questions have to be asked:

- What kind of residential care are we talking about? A small home run along family lines is very different from a specialist organisation of any size.

- How will this child benefit by living in a group? Will the advantages outweigh the loss of family life? Will group care meet the child's emotional, physical and special needs, or as many of them as can be met? How will the "racial", cultural, religious and linguistic needs of black and minority ethnic children be met?

Derek, aged 14, who is described in Section 1, had learned to relate to the staff team as parental figures, during his ten years in a children's home. He demonstrated that he felt safe and important as a member of a group. His physical care was hard for even two people to manage. He suffered from a rare syndrome which necessitated strict medical supervision.

Derek was a young person with one white and one black parent; he identified with black staff but was equally at ease with white carers. Religion was of no significance in his life and his parents had not requested a religious upbringing. Probably a family could have been found for Derek in due course, and he might in the end have settled and profited. However, the local authority had to balance the risks of delay, possible failed introductions and disruptions, against the risks of permanent, appropriate institutional care.

- How does residential care now fit in with the long-term plans for the child or young person? Is it clear what kind of agreement is envisaged in terms of time scales, specialist care and support?

The long-term plan for Derek was permanent residence in a community of disabled people with work and leisure opportunities and medical supervision. There would also have to be provision for his deteriorating condition. The local authority hoped to find such a placement for Derek now, and thus avoid another move later.

- Can the child's parents and other relatives work in partnership within a residential setting? Is shared care a possibility? Have all of the contact issues been explored?

According to the OPCS survey,[2] family contact with disabled children who have been in residential care for over two years becomes less and less frequent and regular, as it did in Derek's case. The same is true for children who are not disabled, but the reasons for it may be different. While children with disabilities are more likely to be placed further from their homes because of their specialised needs, they may be less likely to be able to travel, or to communicate with their families independently, or to make their wishes and feelings explicit. Their parents may feel that they have lost the right to remain parents and that it is somehow kinder and better for the child if they withdraw in favour of the experts. When families can no longer cope with a disabled child at home, feelings of loss, grief, anger and guilt may interfere with maintaining strong bonds.[3]

Assessing residential care

We would not place any disabled child with any family for long-term or permanent care without preparation and assessment of what that family has to offer. Even short-term or respite care is usually based on meeting a child's specific needs. Yet we place children with disabilities in residential care without much ado; a vacancy in a group home willing to take the child is often the only goal. It is then not a question of how that establishment can provide for the child, but whether that child satisfies the admission criteria.

THIS is not the right place for them.'
'We are not meeting their needs.'
'We've done all we can for them and now this placement is counter-productive.'
'They're going downhill rather than progressing.'
'They need a family urgently, now.'

For a fostering worker, such pressures are not unusual. As soon as I came into this post, I knew I would be expected to identify the most needy disabled children, inappropriately placed in residential care, and unblock the sticking points which had so far prevented family placements being found for them.

This is a common experience, and not only in the field of disability. In mainstream child care, there is a constant cry from social workers that residential care is not meeting the needs of young people, and that families must be found. In practice, with current staffing levels, families will not be found for every single child identified. Priorities have to be set and the reality accepted that some young people's experience of living away from home will be group care. Disabled children sadly have even less choice. In this context, it is very hard to develop a positive attitude to group care, but at the same time we are aware of the need to develop better residential provision for disabled children.

While I was familiarising myself with local services, I visited the Department's three residential respite units.

31 January 95 *Looked again at the project report. I am struck by the need for good links to be established between the fostering unit, the respite schemes, and the residential units for disabled children. At the moment there are no points of contact between the workers involved in the different aspects of the service, whereas there are both children and carers who cross those boundaries.*

9 February 95 *Had a meeting with the manager of the unit which takes the middle age-group of children. Useful insights into the background of the unit, which used to be a general children's home, and into the staff's attitude to fostering. They have had some negative experiences – situations in which placements have not worked out because, in their view, the potential carers did not have adequate preparation.*

The purchaser/provider split in social services could ensure a better deal for the child. If social work is to be guided and ruled by the economics of the market place, then at least the buyer should be knowledgeable, discerning and always insist on the best quality.

General information

Before giving serious consideration to a residential home, it is as well to ask for all the printed information available which should include a statement of purpose. Glossy brochures do not describe a service more fully and truly than typed sheets in a folder, but the standard of literacy, the areas covered in the presentation and the application of related research, will reveal a great deal. If no such information is available, it is fitting to ask for a written profile of the home, in exchange for a profile of the child in question. The more freely information flows in both directions, the better. It is a promising sign when care staff are eager to know about a child, and we should not resent the time it takes to give, as well as to gather, good information.

Who are the residents?

When children are placed in substitute families, we are concerned about how the child will fit into the existing group and how that group will, in turn, be affected. Age, degrees of disability, gender, ethnicity, length of stay and family contacts equally affect the dynamics of group care, but this is easily overlooked in the effort to secure a place.

> *Jenny was a bright teenager with severe cerebral palsy. She used a wheelchair, and had a major speech impairment. She was able to control electronic devices and was fiercely independent. When she was placed in a small group home with five other teenagers with varying levels of learning difficulties, she became so depressed and sick that she had to be temporarily moved to a hospital. Jenny's yearning for intellectual stimulation had been sacrificed to a vacancy for a wheelchair.*

It is a mistake to presume that children will live harmoniously together because they are all disabled. On the contrary, their disabilities make them even more disparate than other children are, and it could therefore be even more stressful for them to fit comfortably into a group.

Special care

If the provision is specifically for children with disabilities, it still cannot be suitable for all disabled children. Each child has special needs which are different from the next child's; that is why they are special. It may be that a small group home can best meet the needs of some disabled children but that others will require a whole range of aids and adaptations, medical supervision, training, physiotherapy, massage, night attendance, carers with non-speaking communication skills or experts in behaviour therapy.

An initial assessment of any residential home should include a detailed discussion of how the child's special needs would be provided for in an individual care plan. This gives an opportunity to ascertain whether drugs are used to modify behaviour.

Because children with disabilities are particularly vulnerable, protection from all kinds of abuse should be discussed and built into the care plan. A child who is immobile will require different protection from the child who makes inappropriate sexual overtures.

One special need that most disabled children do have in common is the need for extra stimulation and quality attention. It is an essential part of every assessment to observe the interaction between children and staff; a good time to choose is when the children come back from school – and an invitation to stay for tea should not be refused.

They also have felt, on occasions, that the fostering unit is unnecessarily bureaucratic in its approach, and not sufficiently flexible in responding to enquiries about fostering children, particularly from staff members.

We then discussed the difficulties of running a respite unit, when children are regularly placed who need full-time care. This effectively blocks a respite bed, and is also quite unsatisfactory for the child. Further debate is needed.

Asked the manager how he saw my post. He clearly sees it as an opportunity for quicker and more effective recruitment of families. Also he felt it was important to have a link person to connect with and be able to approach about placements. He would welcome being able to talk over the emerging needs of some of the children in the unit.

7 March 95

Visited the hostel caring for the younger children, and also those with profound physical disabilities. Seemed bright and welcoming, with pleasing physical surroundings. However, the staffing levels restrict the quality of care in terms of stimulation for the children. So this unit provides very good physical care and emotional warmth but any child spending significant amounts of time on respite here, or indeed full-time, would be deprived of the stimulation and individual attention they need – particularly important for the many severely disabled children they care for.

15 March 95

Visited the unit for the older children and young people. An old building – previously an elderly person's home I think. They have been working hard to make it welcoming and suited to their purpose and it still had a feeling of "work in progress" about it. I found it difficult on this visit to gain a real feel of the unit, but it was a time when no residents were in, so I need to plan another visit.

16 March 95

Visited a project which is currently in the middle of a total changeover. It used to be a residential unit, which was created specifically to bring back three young people with extremely challenging behaviour, from placements outside the district and care for them in house. Those young people eventually moved into the community with back-up from the staff. The project is now developing into an outreach team offering support to families or other carers looking after disabled children or young people with very difficult behaviour. This may be a useful resource to remember when I'm setting up placements or hear of placements which are struggling.

Also had a meeting to discuss recruitment of families for Andrew and Gary with the social worker and the residential staff. This followed a couple of months of to-ing and fro-ing between me and various colleagues within the Disability Division following rumours that there were a number of potential families for the boys but nothing was being done about it. This meeting clarified what the situation really was, and also came up with some clear plans about publicity and recruitment. There is indeed one family specifically interested in offering a home to one of the boys, now that the decision has been reached to place them separately. They have made contact with the fostering unit and they are "in the system". No other family has come forward. We looked at a few issues:

a) timing – this is complex because of having to recruit a family from scratch for Gary while having identified one for Andrew. Everyone agreed that it would be undesirable to place one and leave the other in residential care waiting for a family that may never appear. We agreed to try to work towards simultaneous placements if at all possible.

b) recruiting a family for Gary – the unit manager was very optimistic that there would definitely be "a family out there" if they knew of the need. He felt that we should specifically target those who have experience of working with disabled people. In disability terms, these boys are quite easy to care for, particularly on an individual basis.

c) agreed that residential staff would draw up a pen-picture for us to use in our recruitment efforts.

d) agreed to send the information to special schools, respite carers, foster carers and residential units for both children and adults.

A large Victorian manor house had been turned into a home for disabled children. It was one of the few to accept children in wheelchairs with total dependency needs. There was a devoted, long serving staff team led by a qualified residential worker who had been a matron in a hospital. This staff team was supported by a host of agency workers. The home was clean, bright and well appointed for wheelchairs.

When the children returned from school in a special bus, they were each met, brought into the playroom, their outer garments and shoes were removed, slippers were put on, they were made comfortable in their wheelchairs or told to sit on colourful plastic furniture, they were helped to have a drink and a biscuit, and then the television was turned on. There was no chat with the grown ups, and although the children were probably familiar with most of the agency workers, there was apparently no attempt to assign a specific worker to any one child; it was more a matter of first off the bus, first served. It was quiet in the playroom; all the children seemed to be compliant and contented. The workers stayed close at hand to assist.

Tea time was efficiently organised and the food was plentiful and wholesome. The children were encouraged to have pleasant table manners, which included not speaking while they ate. The helpers ate with them. After tea, there was more television until bed-time, which was staggered according to age. Each child had a private cubicle in a dormitory, with a different soft toy on the bed and a different poster on the wall. There were a few photographs on some dressing tables; everything else was neatly put away.

In another smaller home for children with a variety of disabilities, coming back from school was chaotic. The more able children helped the hard pressed staff to bring the children in wheelchairs in from the bus. There was one key worker for every three children; clearly more hands were needed. Everyone talked at once and there was much noise and laughter. It took forever to get all the coats off and not all the slippers could be found. Drinks and biscuits were offered and then some children chose to watch television while another group played games with two workers, and a third group helped to lay the table in an unconventional manner.

Tea was a time for talking about the events of the day. Everyone got a turn including the staff. Table manners were not a priority; drinks were spilled and crumbs went on the floor. After tea one of the carers played requests on an upright piano; some children sang, some danced, and some just clapped hands. One child became over-excited, over-tired, quarrelsome and tearful.

Bedtime was a spread out, one-to-one routine. The key workers put their children to bed whenever possible, but all the staff knew and observed each child's individual bed-time ritual. The shared bedrooms looked like treasure coves. They were overcrowded with toys, pictures, souvenirs from outings, books, cosmetics, trophies and ornaments. Each child's corner reflected a special interest: miniature dolls, teddy bears, model cars, marbles of all colours and sizes, toy aliens, glass animals, or a collection of badges pinned onto a hessian wall hanging.

There can be no definitive guidance about how to measure one home against the other. The first one described above is well thought of by many local authorities and admired by some parents. The second has been criticised for unreliable hygiene and lack of discipline by its management committee, but it is fiercely defended by parents and social workers. Unfortunately we do not know how the children would compare them both or rate either; we can only assess what we see in relation to their special needs.

An additional aid to assessment is to ask the residential workers to outline what might be a weekly diary for the child. Are there outside activities? Do music, art, drama, swimming, shopping, the local library and youth clubs feature in the programme? And if they do not, why not?

This discussion underlined the importance of working closely with residential staff at all stages of recruitment, preparation and support of new families for disabled children. They are key people in describing children and their needs, and they may also have good ideas about finding families. All the residential staff I have met in this job have been keen to find more appropriate settings for the children in their care. It is sometimes the case that residential staff are negative about the prospect of a move to a family, in which case they will need support to enable them to relinquish their care and give the new family permission to take over. Particularly strong attachments can develop between workers and very dependent children. This needs to be acknowledged and valued. The task of transferring these attachments is very similar to work with foster carers of a baby or toddler moving to adopters.

Warner Interviews

This post gave me an opportunity to be involved in the Warner interviews. These are personal interviews which have been introduced for jobs in residential care with children as part of the selection process following the recommendations of the Warner Report[1] into the abuse of children in residential care. I have done a number of joint interviews and this experience prompted me to look at the thinking behind the process and the interview schedule.

16 March 95 Have been involved in four Warner interviews in the last couple of days. I found them very interesting, but have some concerns about the format and the aims which seem a bit fudged. I'd like more clarity. Must discuss with my co-interviewer.

28 March 95 Meeting to discuss the Warner interviews with my co-interviewer, John. Fed back my concerns and we looked at the original thinking and how the current structure came about. It is rather unclear who, if anyone, has overall responsibility for implementing the Warner recommendations and reviewing the procedures to see if they are proving effective. Agreed that I would do some more thinking and look at the Warner Report itself, while John would track down the accountability within the department.

6 May 95 Have done further work on Warner. Studied a copy of the report and its recommendations. I feel some of the assumptions are over-optimistic, if not naive, ie. the assumption that a social worker with fostering assessment skills would be able to glean enough from an initial interview to assess whether someone was a potential abuser.

Also contacted the local project working with perpetrators to see what information they might have re: profiles of abusers, research, etc. They will send me information.

6 June 95 The info from The Perpetrators' Project has arrived. Very interesting research material[2] from interviews with convicted perpetrators.

Offenders were interviewed about the methods they use to target children, the age range of their victims, how they select children and maintain them as victims, and what suggestions they have for preventing child sexual abuse. The men's ages ranged from 19 to 74. Some of the answers were revealing:

– The offenders who themselves had been sexually abused were more inclined to abuse boys than girls. Those offenders who said they had not been abused were much more likely to target girls.

– The vast majority (66 per cent) of the offenders knew their victims through family or friends or caretaking, such as babysitting.

– 49 per cent of the offenders were attracted to children who seemed to lack confidence or were low in self-esteem.

– To find children who might become victims, 36 per cent of the men frequented schools, shopping centres, arcades, playgrounds, parks, beaches, swimming baths, fairs, etc. They worked on becoming welcome in the child's home (33 per cent). It is highly significant that 48 per cent of the offenders found their victims through babysitting.

The staff

Without resorting to inquisitorial methods, we must find out who the residential workers are, and how the staff structure operates. Who is in charge of what, accountable to which body and supervised by whom? What is the staff turnover? What is the worker–child ratio, is there a key worker system, how does the staff rota work, and what happens when the key worker is off duty? Getting the lines of communication straight at this point can save much aggravation later.

We should try to understand the prevailing staff attitudes towards discipline, sex, privacy, mainstream and special education, and independence for children with disabilities. If the child is from a minority ethnic group, will the staff be aware of special dietary rules, festivals, customs, and dress regulations?

Unlike substitute families, residential workers must expect to explain themselves and the service they offer. A frank exchange of views among professionals, or a thorough appraisal by parents, ought to be regarded as a positive step towards making a good placement.

Contact

Philippa Russell, the Director of the Council for Disabled Children writes: 'A particular cause of concern with regard to children with disabilities "looked after" by the local authority is the difficulty they may experience in sharing any concerns or anxieties about their lives.

'... They have fewer informal opportunities to make friends and new contacts, and so the family is crucial in helping them to determine their place in the world and for acting as an advocate when required.'[4]

How can residential services ensure that disabled children maintain contact with their parents, siblings and other relatives, even if they appear not to need it or to benefit by it?

Phil Youdan, the Principal Development Officer of the Residential Care Unit at the National Children's Bureau, has devised some good practice indicators for contact arrangements,[5] which I have adapted to fit the needs of disabled children and their families.

- Information for parents should include details about the arrangements for contact, the name of the staff member responsible, the name of the supervisor, an out of hours telephone number, what role the parents will continue to have in respect of their child, how these arrangements are to be monitored, and how the complaints procedure works.

- Parents should be kept informed on a regular basis about their child's progress, particularly about their education, health and social development in relation to their disability.

- There should be regular meetings between the carers, the parents and the child, if appropriate, at times convenient to the family.

- Parents should be treated with respect, as partners who can still share in their child's care, even if they cannot look after the child at home or cope with the child's disability. Their visits should be valued and they should be encouraged to join in the routines of the establishment, for example, meal times, planning holidays, fundraising events, outings, school related activities, dental and medical examinations and shopping for their own children's clothes.

- Parents should be encouraged to share in occasions which are of importance to the child, like birthdays, religious festivals, prize givings and sports days.

- It is often necessary to offer families help with transport arrangements. Lifts to and from stations or bus stops can give a welcoming signal.

- The offenders carefully tested the child's reaction to sex by bringing up sexual matters or having sexual material around, and then used subtle increasing sexual touching (50 per cent).
– 60 per cent of the abusers worried about the child disclosing.
– 50 per cent said that the child saying no or displaying fear, crying, being sad or in pain or distress would make them uncomfortable. However, only 26 per cent said they would stop the abuse.

This kind of research material does not provide us with any specific information in terms of the profile of potential abusers, but it does help me to remain alert to the fact that abusers target vulnerable children, and that disabled children must be in a high risk category. I am less and less convinced we can achieve anything in the initial personal interview – other aspects of practice and monitoring seem more important eg. instituting "safe caring" policies. Still, Warner may help us to sharpen up our practice, making it easier for staff, or relatives, to "blow the whistle" when the child is being cared for away from home. These issues are equally important in family placement.

7 August 95
Meeting re: Warner interviews. Very useful discussion with colleagues who also interview. Fed back where I was on the original report, research, and the local Perpetrators' Project. Discussed how we might re-design the guidance on these interviews so that it is more effectively included in the recruitment process, and that this is made explicit to the applicants.

20 November 95
Involvement in more Warner interviews over the last three days. I found it worked very much better with the newly designed process which has now been agreed.

Extract from a memo recommending new guidelines for these interviews:

Personal interviews have generated a great deal of concern both in candidates and staff alike. "Grapevine" accounts of interrogations about people's sexual preferences and activities have abounded – not helped by references to "paedophile" or "pervert" interviews. However, in spite of expressed concerns, no individual complaints have been received by the personnel section about this part of the process. Nevertheless, it must be seen to be open to scrutiny. Experience has indicated that it is the skills and experience of interviewers that elicit relevant information rather than any one set of questions. Staff involved believed that the interviews have been worthwhile in identifying candidates who would be vulnerable in residential settings. No claim is made that determined abusers have been identified in this process.

A panel should be established from which people could be drawn to undertake preliminary interviews – the panel to include:
– Black staff
– a mix of men and women
– staff with disabilities
– staff who have undertaken recruitment and selection training
– staff with extensive interview experience
– staff with experience in child protection work/work with perpetrators
– staff who have studied and applied theories of human growth and development

This group could meet together for supervision and development and be accountable to a named manager. Discussions need to take place about possible systems for monitoring recruitment outcome including appointments and subsequent disciplinary action.

- Parents and other family members should be encouraged to keep the staff informed of any changes in their circumstances or about significant family events which may have an impact on the wellbeing of the child.

- Children and young people in residential care must have access to a private telephone, supplies of writing paper and stamps; children with disabilities may require sensitive assistance to use them. Private mail should not be opened or read, unless the children are completely incapable of doing it themselves. If a child has to be protected from threatening family members, staff should support the child to deal with an unwelcome letter, but should not withhold it.

These practice points make a formidable list for discussing and assessing an organisation's attitude towards disabled children's families, openness and contact. The expectations are high, but it cannot be stressed too often that being disabled and away from home should never lead to becoming disconnected. The 1989 Children Act (paragraph 17 of Schedule 2) places a duty on local authorities to appoint an Independent Visitor if a child does not have sufficient contact with parents or others with parental responsibility. An Independent Visitor could provide a valuable link with home for disabled children who are placed at a great distance from their families.[6] Another item on the agenda!

Support, reviews and liaison

Finding and agreeing a suitable residential provision for a disabled child is not a one-way process. The residential staff and management also have to make an assessment: they have to balance the needs of the children already in their care with the demands the new child would make on time and resources. Gender, age, ethnicity and disability will have to be taken into account. They have to judge whether they would be able to work with the child's family and with the child's social workers; and they have to consider how their organisation would fit into the long-term care plan. Can they offer

permanence? Are they equipped and willing to prepare a disabled child to move back home or to a substitute family or to an independent unit?

The most carefully chosen residential establishment will not be able to give of its best unless supported by the social workers who have placed the children. Support means sharing information, being available, visiting regularly, keeping appointments, fixing reviews at convenient times, producing prompt and correct minutes of meetings, and keeping abreast of the child's progress and disability. It also means helping staff to carry out difficult plans, such as parting with a child who is to be adopted or allowing contact with a parent who is disruptive.

Support and liaison have to be built in from the beginning; a written agreement should specify who will be responsible for liaison, who will deputise, who will supervise, who will visit, and who will review. What will be the out of hours cover? If social workers leave, a case involving a disabled child in residential care should be the first and not the last to be reallocated.

Residential schools

As residential homes continue to close, local authorities are forced to find alternative placements for children with disabilities who for one reason or another cannot, or should not, be placed with substitute families. There is a trend for boarding schools to offer a service for 52 weeks of the year or to contract out to a variety of respite and holiday provision, thus re-enacting the role of residential homes. If children are "looked after" by local authorities, a boarding school for children with disabilities should be assessed as carefully, including the holiday arrangements, as any other residential placement. However, a mutually rewarding partnership with an education department can be hard to establish and harder to maintain. Boarding schools are traditionally independent and exclusive. Many specialise in specific disabilities with an almost national catchment area, so that children may have to be placed in remote country districts and far away from their families and social workers.

Parents' perspective

In my contact with parents of disabled children, both individually and in groups, some general themes have emerged about their views of residential care.

For some parents, residential care is a more acceptable alternative because it is easier to accept that "experts" can care for their child when they cannot. Also, one group of Asian mothers felt that although they could use family placements for day care, it would be unacceptable within their community for another family to take on overnight care – if this was needed, it had to be residential care.

Parents whose children present very challenging behaviour found that residential respite care has proved the only reliable option. Some tried a series of family placements which failed and understandably they now prefer the reliability of residential provision.

Most parents preferred hospital or hospice care for profoundly disabled or terminally ill children.

Residential school was a popular option for some parents who were finding full-time care of their child too demanding, but who did not like the stigma of either fostering or residential care.

I believe that many of these views can be changed if there is good contact between disability and fostering units and a willingness to work together. A recent example of this is recorded in the following diary entry.

19 June 96 Visit from a disability social worker to discuss the case of Sam, a two-year-old who is profoundly disabled and has been in hospital for the last six months. His parents are very reluctant to take him home – they had been told he would not live beyond the age of one and have essentially run out of the energy and commitment needed to care for him. They would prefer him to stay in hospital, or perhaps go to a residential school.

One of the alternatives we considered was a shared care arrangement which might enable the parents both to hold on to and let go of John – the worker wasn't sure but thought she could discuss this with them. Luckily, one of our most experienced foster carers of disabled young children is about to have a vacancy because one of her foster children is moving to adoptive parents.

The link worker from the Adoption and Fostering Unit was available for a brief discussion. He felt it would be a suitable placement for Sam, and this foster carer would be excellent in building a relationship with the birth parents. She is very understanding and non-judgemental. So I arranged for the two workers to liaise further.

21 August 96 Read *Gone Missing*[3] a research document produced by the Who Cares? Trust. Very moving and distressing accounts from disabled adults of their experiences of living away from their families of origin.

It is difficult to comment realistically from the child's perspective on the services we provide for them. We are still a long way in most child care organisations (particularly statutory ones) from really listening to the voice of the child. If this is true of the general population of "looked after" children, then how about those disabled children who have even more obstacles in the way of having their voices heard? I found this report extremely helpful in reminding me of the child's point of view, and the constant need to monitor what is happening in their lives when they are in residential care. We should all vow not to allow Jake's story (on the following page) to be repeated in this or any future generation of disabled children.

Undisputed expertise, waiting lists and high reputations tend to make us feel grateful if a child is offered a place; but feeling grateful should not make us forget our responsibilities to disabled children who cannot fend for themselves. And we know from children without disabilities that they can be miserable at boarding school for many years. That is not to say that boarding schools are miserable places, but that we should not assume that they are the right place for a disabled child without further exploration.

Long stay hospitals

The National Health Service continues to have a role in the total care of some of the most severely disabled children. Very few of these are "looked after" by local authorities. NHS establishments may offer respite services to both families and local authorities, but there should be no queston of allowing the respite to become a long-term residential placement. The Department of Health guidelines are very clear on this point.[7]

Conclusion

I am well aware of the discrepancies between how it should be, and how it is out there in the real world. Many local authorities seem to have no choice about residential placements and the very idea of assessing a residential home will be ridiculed. But that can lead to a counsel of despair on the one hand and to undervalued residential care on the other.

References

1. Kahan B, *Growing up in Groups*, HMSO, 1994.
2. Office of Population and Census Surveys, *Surveys of Disability in the UK, Report 3, Prevalence of Disability among Children*, 1989.
3. Russell P, 'The Importance of Contact for Children with Disabilities' in Argent H (ed), *See You Soon – Contact with children who are looked after by local authorities*, BAAF, 1996.
4. See 3 above.
5. Youdan P, 'Hello Mum, Hello Dad' in Argent H (ed), *See You Soon – Contact with children who are looked after by local authorities*, BAAF, 1996.
6. See 3 above.
7. Department of Health, *Children Act Guidelines and Regulations, Volume 6, Children with Disabilities,* HMSO, 1991.

I was born in 1960 and at the age of two I was hospitalised, basically because there was nowhere else to go and they wanted to find out what was wrong with me. Then my father died and my mother was left with my two brothers and two sisters to look after. She had no choice but to put me in residential care. There were just no facilities for disabled children.

When I was two and a half they put me in another hospital where there was no medical care but where they just looked after you. I was there for 16 years. There was no talk of fostering or adopting because my family were around. But no-one talked about helping my mother look after me at home. She didn't have the support, she couldn't afford to stay home from work – she had to work because my father had died. What was talked about was what would happen when I reached the age of 16 – where was the next dumping ground?

I went into a Cheshire Home because there was nowhere else for me to go. Then I went to a residential further education college for two and a half years. In some ways it was a break from institutional life but when I left there the only choice was residential care. I recently did a training course for disabled people at a further education college and for some people there, the only thing on offer when they leave is still more residential care.

After I left the college, there was no other option but to go to another residential home. I thought it was the end of my life. But I made a promise to myself that I would do whatever I could to get out of there within two years. It took six years before I finally got a place of my own to live and the funding for the support I need.

(Jake's story from *Gone Missing?*)

Thankfully, independent living is becoming a possible choice for disabled people, although progress is slow. But Jake's story of his experience of residential care is neither the only one nor the worst. We must learn to provide more than bed, board and shelter for disabled children and young people – they deserve better, and residential care deserves to be less ill-used.

References

1. *Choosing with Care – Report of the Committee of Inquiry into the Selection, Development and Management of Staff in Children's Homes*, Chairman Norman Warner, HMSO, 1997.
2. Elliott M, *Child Sexual Abuse Prevention: What offenders tell us*, Kidscape Charity for Children's Safety, 1995.
3. Morris Dr J, *Gone Missing? A research and policy review of disabled children living away from their families*, Who Cares? Trust, 1995.
4. See 3 above.

Working with **disabled children** before, during and after **placement**

Gathering information

Before the needs of identified children who require substitute or additional care can be assessed, all the information available about each child must be collected and collated:

- up-to-date medical reports from GP, developmental specialist, expert in specific disability and health visitor;
- school reports, educational psychologist's report, copy of educational statement or record in Scotland;
- reports from speech, art, play and physio-therapists, as appropriate;
- discussion with any other key professionals as indicated;
- detailed family background including medical history;
- photographic record of child, child's family and previous carers;
- child's life story filled out with memories by family and carers;
- "a day in the life of the child" recorded in writing or on cassette by current carer;
- significant people in child's life; contact needs in short and long term, parents' ability to sustain contact and contribute to placement;
- child's capacity to attach, need to regress, degree of institutionalisation, experience of separation and loss;
- financial support available.

This is no doubt a daunting list preaching a counsel of perfection. But it should go a long way towards an understanding of the whole child and of the child's needs in placement.

What do children with disabilities have a right to expect?

Information and explanation according to their age and level of comprehension

It is not possible or desirable to approach children with disabilities as a homogeneous group. A twelve-year-old with a physical disability could be intellectually advanced for his age, a child of fourteen with severe learning difficulties could have the understanding of a four-year-old, and a child with minor disabilities could be seriously held back by emotional problems. But no child who has to be introduced to substitute family or residential care, is too disabled to be informed about what is going to happen in some way they can understand.

Wise parents do not take their toddler on an aeroplane without explaining that they will fly in the air, but they surely will not go on to explain aerodynamics, although a little information about seatbelts, length and purpose of the trip, funny feelings in the ears, and food available on the way, would not come amiss. If the toddler has a disability, the parents will be sensitive about any special provisions needed for the journey. When the child is older, the explanations and information can be more technical, but the purpose will be the same: to allay anxiety about the unknown and to allow the child to have some control during the journey.

Children who have to separate from their parents are truly going on a journey, and if they are disabled, it is an extra factor to take into account when designing each child's package of travel information.

Drawings, puppets, a doll's house, stories, games and meeting other children with the same disability in similar situations, will often be more meaningful than words alone.[1] Most children enjoy a tour of the office: meeting the team, seeing their own file, and working the photocopier gives them confidence in the service.

Nearly all children want to know at some level, although they may not be able to ask at any level, the answers to the following questions.

- What exactly is my disability and what does it mean?
- Why do I need another family? Is it because I am disabled?
- What is adoption, respite or foster care?
- What is a residential home?
- What is this agency, how does it work, who are the workers?
- Why must I have my photo taken? What is publicity?
- Are there other children like me? What happened to them?
- Will I still see my mum, dad, auntie, gran, brother, dog, cat and anyone else I want to see?

Before beginning work with a disabled child, it is essential to know how questions have been answered by the parents or carers. Work can only progress if it starts from where the child is.

Daniel, aged twelve, had a kidney disease. He did not know how serious it was, because he had been in care since he was four and no-one had told him. His mother, whom he saw infrequently, and the residential staff wanted to protect him from the painful truth. His condition became worse soon after he was referred for adoption. The family placement worker had to move carefully from what Daniel could remember of hospital visits and being sick, to his present medical prognosis, which included the probability of dialysis and a kidney transplant. When a family was found, Daniel, now fourteen, took pride in teaching his prospective adopters about kidney disease.

8 March 95 *From the beginning, I have been determined to focus on the children's perspective and to concentrate on their needs.*

Considering the issue of direct work with disabled children and what role I might have in this, my initial thoughts are:
– My responsibility is primarily as planner, developer.
– The only direct work I do is with adults.
– But all work, including strategic development, must keep the needs of the child in the foreground.
– Build in structures which enable workers and carers to do good quality work with children.
– Who should do this work?
social worker?
foster carer?
residential worker?
– Need to work on individual plan for each child, with clear aims and purpose.
– Look at well-established principles of working with children and adapt methods to take account of any specific disability.
– Talk to workers and carers who are doing this work.
– One of the things which strikes me immediately is the increased vulnerability of disabled children, their dependence on carers/parents to speak for them, protect them, ensure good quality care. True of all children to an extent, but a child without speech can't phone Childline.
– My role as Development Officer is to develop my own thinking first, then act as a catalyst to bring about the necessary debate with workers, both within the mainstream and disability services.

15 June 95 *I met Peter ... quite an experience! Peter stole the show really – not much else happens when he is in the room – he tends to be the centre of attention, very much like a toddler. He certainly explored me – I'll wear trousers the next time I go. He's a very physical child, clambered on me, touched me, pinched me, grabbed my handbag and proceeded to empty it: constantly wanted to play.*

Continuity

Whether children with disabilities are accommodated, come into the care system, or have respite placements away from home, they have a right to expect that continuity will be preserved for them. Even if they cannot express the need for contact or cannot show pleasure when it takes place, the loss of continuity is a further handicap which must be avoided. If siblings have to be separated from their parents, they ought not to be also separated from each other; if only one sibling has disabilities there will probably be intertwined feelings of dependency and responsibility which must not be ignored. It is not always easy to help children to stay in touch with their past; when children do not read or write, are unable to use the telephone, to walk or to travel unaided, then it is both more difficult and more important to help them. A child with a learning impairment might otherwise assume that people and the past disappear, or a child with a physical impairment might deduce that disability destroys relationships.

Some aids for continuity

- Contact which is not only direct contact with parents and others. Siblings, grandparents, relatives, friends, neighbours, previous teachers and carers can keep in touch by sending post cards, gifts, messages on tape, photographs and drawings.[2] It is clearly essential that the current carers are in agreement with every detail of contact, however indirect or irregular, because the success of the arrangement will depend on their support.

- Life story work, provided it is not a once and for all effort produced to impress new carers.[3] The point about life story work should be that it is the child's never ending story which includes absent family and friends. All kinds of materials can be used to record life stories: videos, cassettes, a roll of parchment, a series of wallposters, diaries, and of course a book bought for the purpose, but preferably not a flimsy scrap book which will fall to pieces.

The life story does not have to be neat, legible or in strictly chronological order; anecdotes are as good as facts, but it is not a fairy story and must tell the truth, for instance, about disability, separation and loss. Anything that is meaningful to the child should be put in, including a sweet wrapper or a bus ticket if it triggers a memory. The work has to appeal to the child and to the carer, so that they can record a living history together, in which the past and present mingle.

It could be that a child is too disabled to participate and seems not to respond when the story is read or shown; even so, it may hold a meaning.

Seven-year-old Donald, who was mycrocephalic and had multiple disabilities, would not be separated from his life story. He tore all other books but not this one. Although he could certainly not comprehend the story, he knew it was his. Because it was valued, he was proud of himself. He turned the pages carefully and pointed at the pictures and laughed.

- Address books, autograph books, framed photographs, treasured belongings and anything at all that is connected to the past. It is not a case of staying stuck in the past, but if the connections are broken, the move forward will be hazardous.

- Visits to places the child has known: the house where the child lived when a baby, the hospital where he had his operation, her first school, the park where he got lost.

Sally, aged eleven, had seen her single mother taken away in an ambulance and knew she was dead because people said so. Sally had learning difficulties and no concept of death. She was not taken to the funeral because no-one wanted to upset her. As far as she was concerned, her mother had not come back because she was cross. Only much later, when she was taken to see the grave, did she understand why her mother could not look after her any longer. She could then begin to relate to her dead mother and to move into the future.

16 June 95 Reflecting on yesterday's meeting with Peter, I am wondering how to work with him given his limitations in understanding the world, eg. he can say very few words but has no difficulty in communicating what he wants. So, if he wants a drink, he will take you and put your hand on the juice bottle. However, his understanding of what is being said to him is much greater than his ability to speak (like a pre-verbal child).

24 April 96 At Peter's review yesterday, care workers and his teacher all commented that Peter has coped remarkably well in the last 6 months with a number of major changes – his respite unit was being refurbished so he has had to adapt to a move to temporary accommodation. He has remained settled and happy, with no re-emergence of his challenging behaviour, such as biting and hitting children and some members of staff. His school has merged with another school and his peer group has changed substantially. There has been a very unsettled atmosphere in the school. Peter has remained calm and happy in this environment.

A number of features have probably helped Peter to cope well with these changes:
– clear, simple explanations of what is happening
– continuity of key adults in both settings.

Despite the major changes, Peter has been one of the constant children in his group, giving him security and status. At school, he and a few other children stayed with the same teacher, while more students joined the group. Similarly, in the residential unit, he was one of a small group of children receiving high levels of respite care who were given priority and remained together in the move to temporary accommodation.

8 May 96 We must use Peter's previous experience in our plans for the move to his shared care family. He is already visiting Jackie and Ian in their house. Now we must talk to him about staying there instead of the residential unit.

However, timing is crucial. We can't introduce the idea too soon or he'll be confused and unsettled if it doesn't happen quickly. So we continue to build up his confidence with the new people and in the new place. Once the approval process and the practicalities such as adaptations to the house are complete, then all the key people in his life will reinforce the message that he will be going to stay at Jackie's house instead of the residential unit. The details will be sorted out in a planning meeting, so that we can agree what words will be used and other aids to communication, such as photos, drawings – so that there is consistency for Peter. In enabling this process, I shall be particularly keen to listen to those people who know Peter best and understand how he makes sense of his world. I will have a framework, and a variety of ideas, but the details of the plan will come from the important people in Peter's life.

5 June 96 PLANNING MEETING met with Julia (Peter's mother), Jackie, Bob, and me.[5] The purpose of the meeting was to plan the placement, now that it has been approved by the Fostering Panel. The move will probably happen quite quickly once everyone agrees we are ready.

We all feel Peter would not cope well with a gradual shift from the residential unit to the family, for example, staying one night the first week and gradually building up to the final three nights per week. The primary task of familiarising Peter with Jackie and Ian will be through the daytime weekly visits which have already started. In a previous move from one residential unit to another, it was found that Peter could not cope with a gradual move ie. starting with one overnight stay. He found it too confusing. So we decided that as soon as Peter shows he is quite at home and comfortable with Jackie and her surroundings, he will leave the residential unit and transfer to Jackie and Ian for shared care.

To summarise: the information and explanations we are giving to Peter about his situation at the moment are based on well-established principles of openness, honesty and clarity in our work with children. The methods we are using are based on the experiences of those people already closely involved in Peter's life and our own previous experience of helping Peter to understand and cope with change.

Protection

If children have been abused, they have a right to expect that they will not be hurt again. Children with disabilities are especially vulnerable: they may be unable to defend themselves or to understand the implications and paradoxes of sexual abuse. They have to be protected from face-to-face contacts which could possibly be dangerous.[4] A delicate balance has to be found between keeping connections alive, trusting the carers, and keeping the child safe.

Respect for "race", religion and culture

There is every reason to assume that children with even the most severe learning difficulties are aware of their own and other people's skin colour.

> *Jason, a black baby with multiple disabilities, was placed with a white foster carer soon after birth. When he was two years old he was placed for adoption with a single black parent. He repeatedly touched his own skin and then stroked his new mother's face with real pleasure.*

Racism may be an added burden for disabled children, which they are less well equipped to deal with than other children.[5]

I have heard it said that it is hard enough to find families for children with disabilities, without limiting choice by imposing racial, religious or cultural matching. It could be said that it is hard enough to be disabled in a substitute family, without having to deal with racial, religious or cultural clashes. Even if a disabled child appears to remain undisturbed by differences, the child's birth family will be aware of them, and if they disapprove it will affect the child. Dietary laws, rules of hygiene and dress, traditions, rituals and festivals can draw people together or set them apart.

> *Janine was a young teenager with Down's Syndrome. She came from a large, overburdened family with the strong religious beliefs and strict observances of Jehovah's Witnesses. Whenever the family asked for respite care, Janine went to stay in a children's home where little was understood about her religion in spite of the parent's attempts to educate the staff. They felt that Janine was somehow contaminated every time she went there, and they found it painful to keep in touch when she went away. Consequently the staff regarded them as uncaring parents and included Janine in activities which she liked, but which alienated her further from her family. They disapproved of the activities, and blamed Janine for wanting to participate.*
>
> *The crunch came when Janine asked to spend Christmas, which the family did not celebrate, in the children's home because she had been promised treats and presents. The parents withdrew Janine from the respite care scheme and suffered in silence. Finally, a preacher from their own community found carers who were willing to have Janine on a regular basis. The two families understood and trusted each other, and while they shared Janine's care, they joined together to celebrate their religion and affirm their culture. However unconcerned with religion Janine remained, this was a more wholesome experience for her than the fragmentation resulting from her respite care in the children's home.*

Janine's family were Christians although they belonged to a minority sect. But not all children and their families are Christians. Many do not observe Christmas and Easter because they are Hindus or Moslems or Jews. They do not have Christian names and they are never christened. They worship other gods and follow other customs. The disability factor does not mean that the parents' or the carers' belief systems can be safely ignored.

There will be some cases where one need will conflict with another; if specialised care is a priority, and a qualified nurse is ready to give up her job in order to care for the child at home, and she is in all other respects the front runner, then the issue of religion or ethnicity might have to take second place.

Thoughts about Rosie

Rosie is a very different child in a different situation. What approach would we take and what differences would there be in working with her? She has no speech, decreasing mobility, is totally dependent on others for all her needs, and has very few ways of letting people know what she wants or is feeling.

Because we have not yet succeeded in finding her a family for shared care, Rosie has recently started to attend a residential unit for respite care. We shall be using our knowledge of what has and has not worked in introducing her to that setting when we prepare her for another family, if we find one.

Her parents would talk to her about the plan in terms they think she would understand, for example, using whatever stories they can find about people moving or living in two different places. Listening to stories is one of Rosie's favourite pastimes. If we can't find anything suitable, we'll have to write something ourselves. Maybe Rosie's sisters would like to be involved in that.

One aspect of working closely with Rosie's family may be that it will also provide them with a way of preparing themselves for the reality. Often, when we are faced with the challenge of presenting complex issues to children, it can help us to unravel some of that complexity, go back to basics, and gain a better understanding ourselves – even, at times to see where we have gone wrong, where we need to be more flexible, or perhaps change our approach.

If we are arranging to move a child with very little mobility, speech, or sensory ability, then we must be extra vigilant to provide continuity of the things that contain meaning and form that child's perception of their world. So ways of lifting, handling, giving intimate bodily care, and talking to the child must be rigorously observed by new carers and followed as closely as possible. Introducing a child like Rosie, might mean the new carer visiting her home and working alongside her parents to "learn the ropes" before any more could be planned.

We all need to stretch our imaginations when working with a disabled child, to really try to "get inside their skin" and imagine the world from their perspective. Of course, birth or adoptive parents and current carers will be crucial in teaching us how to achieve individual plans which really do provide continuity.

Comparing need

Peter and Rosie

Looking at the two children in the pilot shared care scheme, their need for continuity is the same but the challenges they present to preserve that continuity are very different.

Peter is mobile, already has experience of living in different places and adjusting to different settings. He can communicate his wants and needs quite effectively. He is maturing and slowly gaining more skills and abilities.

Rosie is totally physically dependent, has always lived at home with her family, is gradually losing abilities due to her condition, and has less repertoire to communicate her needs and feelings. She is, however, used to a lot of different people caring for her.

For Peter, continuity will include clear explanation, direct experience of new surroundings, seeing the adults spending time together and having a co-ordinated approach. Most of the familiarisation will be done at the new carer's house.

In contrast, Rosie's initial encounter with a new family will probably be within her own home, while they learn all about her physical care, routines and idiosyncracies. They will need to learn from the parents and gradually build up their own confidence.

An important area of work with Peter is to ensure similar responses from home, school and respite unit to a whole range of behaviour, from outbursts of temper to toileting habits. Any new carer will need to be included in the teamwork approach or Peter will become very confused.

The same is true for Rosie – she will scream and scream if things happen in the wrong order – woe betide you if you try to give Rosie her tea when she knows it's her usual time for watching a video!

However, a transracial placement can still be a racially aware placement, and a same race befriender or relation can then fill the gaps and sustain the links. Ethnicity, religion and culture always matter, but the more complex the needs of children with disabilities, the more does one need have to be weighed against another.

> *Billy was born with Ascot's Syndrome, which is an extremely rare condition. He was born without eyelids, external ears, lips or a proper nose. His Irish mother and African-Caribbean father abandoned him in hospital and were never heard of again. Billy survived many operations, and plastic surgery provided him with a functional, if very patchy, and startling face. He was kept more or less shielded from public view in a residential hospital with educational facilities for children with disabilities. But an enlightened nursing sister sent him to the village school and introduced the world to him.*
>
> *When he was seven, Billy was referred for adoption. After a two year search and two bitter disappointments for Billy, the family which was ready to make a lifelong commitment to him was white. The local authority had a "same race" placement policy, although they had allowed him to live all his life with white nursing staff. By this time Billy was desperate to have a family of his own. Opportunities and needs had to be balanced, panels and committees had to be persuaded and arrangements had to be made for Billy to have a black, independent adult visitor when he was placed. This young man become an honorary member of the family and a big brother model for Billy. They went to listen to steel bands together, to eat Caribbean food and to meet other black people including the young man's own family. The Notting Hill Carnival came to be the high point of Billy's year. But he felt he belonged to his white family.*

Preparation to move

Children have a right to expect to be prepared for a move to a family or group home. Hilary Alton's book, *Moving Pictures*,[5] can be adapted

for any age and level of understanding. It offers general themes for discussion and can keep children busy colouring in the chosen pictures of a variety of "care" and "family" situations which include aspects of disability.

Preparation for a specific placement should begin with an exchange of life stories. Families should also write and illustrate a book, send a cassette or a video, and later, a post card to say how much they value the child's story. A residential home should do something similar.

Children have to be reassured that the new carers expect, understand and will be able to manage their disability; especially if their birth family could not manage. Questions they may ask or may wish they could ask, go something like this:

– Do they know I can't walk? Are they strong enough to lift me? Will my wheelchair go in? Have you told them I wet the bed?
– Will they understand me when I speak funny? Do they get cross when things get broken? Will they help me to dress? Will they cope with my fits? Will they give me my injections? Will they stay with me in hospital?
– Will they know sign language? Will they know about braille? Will they have rails in the bathroom?

And the ultimate question:
– What happens if they can't manage?

Reassurance must not be false; children have to know that every placement cannot work every time, but they also have to know that there is always another time and that their disability will not be the cause of disruption.

Planned introductions

Most children get upset when they move to a new house with their own family in the most favourable circumstances. Children who have to leave their homes and their parents to live with a substitute family have very much more to be upset about. No matter how well prepared they have been for a new placement, the actual move will be scary.

Andrew and Gary

Andrew and Gary's needs will have to be very carefully assessed because the decision to place them separately involves a radical plan of discontinuity. They have always lived together, they have lost other siblings, parents and foster carers, but they have been with each other. So we must find ways of sustaining their relationship with each other while meeting their individual needs through separate placements.

Providing continuity for children who have to leave their families of origin, whether through respite, shared, temporary or permanent care, is inextricably linked with helping them to deal with separation and loss. When we place Andrew and Gary separately, we hope to meet their primary need for parenting better than we could do if they stayed together, but we must also acknowledge that they will both suffer in that separation.

Vera Fahlberg's work[1] on separation and loss is clear, accessible and available. We can use it in our work with Andrew and Gary – some of the techniques may need to be adapted and we may have to think up new ones, but we must not neglect the task of working on these issues with disabled children because it seems too daunting. 'They wouldn't understand', often really means 'I can't think how to explain it to them'.

8 May 95 I'm struck by the awareness and fears about abuse voiced by many parents I have spoken to. Comments like these are very common:

'She can't tell us what has happened to her although we feel we'd KNOW somehow, it's still a real worry.' (parents of a 14-year-old girl receiving regular respite care in a residential unit)

'There's always the fear that he might be abused when he's away and we'd never know.' (parents of a 16-year-old boy whose future away from home is being considered)

It is one of the most haunting fears a parent can have and it can sometimes prevent them getting the respite they need. While some parents are convinced they would know if their child had been abused in any way, others feel they would have no way of knowing.

Needs of black disabled children

In Bradford, we have a higher proportion of black carers than the proportion of black to white in the population. But even so we have not got enough placements for black children. If transracial placements have to be made, they are closely monitored and we are constantly trying to address this problem.

We have found too few black foster carers with a special interest in disability, and disabled black children have a high chance of being placed transracially. However, the family-based respite care scheme in Bradford has succeeded in recruiting an adequate number of black families. This is primarily because the scheme has employed black staff from its inception in 1984. But although the Adoption and Fostering Unit also has a good record of employing black staff, the emphasis so far has been on mainstream recruitment. As the only unit worker with a disability focus, and being white, I will certainly need to involve my black colleagues in recruiting black families for disabled children.

Soon after I came to this post, I was asked to advise on a potential shared care situation for a young mixed parentage baby.

9 May 95 Pat (Adoption and Fostering worker) asked me for advice about a child in one of her foster homes. Rebecca is of Asian and white parentage and has severe impairment caused through non-accidental injury inflicted by her mother. She is with a white foster carer and is being rehabilitated to her Asian father. The plan has gone well so far, but the father says he cannot cope with the full-time care of Rebecca and is asking for a period of shared care with the foster family. The area social worker sees this as the best option for the child.

They have a right to expect that introductions will be planned to build up their confidence and to familiarise them with their new carers and surroundings as far as possible. But this does not mean that introductions should be drawn out for an unspecified length of time; children are not reassured if they feel that the adults are also uncertain. The carefully considered and clearly stated aims of each introduction plan should determine the details and the timing.

Points to consider

- Introductions can be very short and very intensive at the same time; children with learning difficulties, or very young children, cope better with brief intervals between meetings and may become confused by repeated visits to the new home.
- Frequent journeys should be avoided for children who have physical disabilities or find travel tiring; distance, escorts, and stamina are deciding factors for planning.
- What does this child see, hear, comprehend, retain and anticipate? There are many ways to familiarise children with new surroundings and to help them to trust new people; touch and smell as well as sight and sound can be creatively used for children with sensory impairments, and food is a universal communicator.
- Shopping expeditions, visits to the park, the zoo, the playground, the public library, car rides, train trips and country walks are good ways to get to know people; children are generally more relaxed on outings than on visits.
- Some children can make the move if they have become used to the new carers, for others the new place is most important.
- The child will gain confidence if the new carers are comfortable with the arrangements.
- Pets are helpful ice breakers – children can confide in a new dog more easily than in a new carer.
- Introduction plans have to be detailed enough to give a firm framework and flexible enough to respond to situations as they arise; in other words, nothing should be left to chance but everything should be negotiable.

- The carers' extended family or other residents from the group home should be included in introductions but not share responsibility for making decisions about the placement.
- Each stage of an introduction has to be monitored; a format for feedback from the child and the carers must be built into the plan.

The right to be heard

All children have a right to be heard, but it can be difficult to hear what children with disabilities have to say. They may not be able to express themselves in words or to speak clearly; they may not understand what is bothering them or they may feel too vulnerable to complain. If there is uncertainty about how a child is feeling or faring, expert guidance from a play therapist, a psychologist or another specialist may be called for (see Appendix E). Support work with disabled children has to continue in placement, whether it is adoption, foster or respite care. It should not be a question of "Can we afford to do it?" We have to ask ourselves if we can afford not to.

Although this section concentrates on work with children with disabilities, there is no dividing line between working with one child and another. All work with children has to be designed to meet individual needs and to match individual capacities; disability is one of many factors which will shape the work.

References

1. Batty D (ed), *Working with Children*, BAAF, 1984.
2. See 1 above.
3. Ryan T and Walker R, *Life Story Work*, BAAF, 1993 .
4. Westcott H, *The Abuse of Children and Adolescents with Disabilities*, NSPCC, 1993.
5. Argent H, *Post-adoption services for children with disabilities*, Paper published by the Post-Adoption Centre, 1996.
6. Alton H, *Moving pictures*, BAAF, 1987.

Issues we need to look at from the unit's perspective are:
– timescales – months or years?
– racial, religious and cultural needs
– payment – will we pay a full-time fee?
Agreed to attend a meeting set up for tomorrow to help sort things out.

10 May 95 Attended meeting at hospital to explore shared care placement for Rebecca. I feel unhappy that the foster carer wants to take this on in addition to the two placements she is approved for. Rebecca's level of need may well escalate rather than decrease, and we must be sure she can receive the intensive care she requires. Agreed that we must pay the full-time fee for shared care. The timescales are a bit unclear, as the father does not know when he might be able to cope with his daughter full-time. This agreement will be for a minimum of six months. When we discussed the child's needs in terms of her "race", religion and culture, we agreed that although an Asian foster home would be preferable, continuity was an overriding need for the baby at the moment, particularly because of her disability. We also felt the regular stays with her father and his input to the foster home were balancing factors.

Looking back, I feel it was a reasonably good decision, but did not take account of the possibility of less and less time being spent with the father, and the foster placement becoming virtually full-time. If this happens we will have created a transracial placement by default.

26 January 96 The more I am involved in working with, thinking about, and trying to write about practice involving disabled children, the less difference I can see from the work with non-disabled children. The message is: don't be paralysed by the child's disabilities. Use the same basic principles as you would in working with any child.

We might have to seek some help about communication skills, or find out about different impairments, but essentially the disabled child's needs are the same as any other child's. We might also have to work towards equality of service for disabled children but we do not require a completely different set of skills or knowledge. The key word is "adapt". Let us adapt our knowledge of child care to the world of the disabled child.

3 June 96 How can I build in monitoring systems to current placements or new ones, whether shared, temporary, or permanent, which assure the right of disabled children to have a say in their lives?

We have a complaints procedure under the provisions of the Children Act to make sure that children who are looked after by the local authority have a voice. How can we make sure disabled children are heard if they are unhappy?

Similarly, within our reviewing procedures, there is always a section for the child's own views to be recorded and taken into account when decisions are made – how do we rise to the challenge of first establishing the views of a disabled child, and then responding?

Specifically thinking about Peter, how have we tried to find out what he might think about the plan to offer him a family placement for shared care, rather than a residential unit? And in future, how will we find out what he thinks of this particular shared care family?

Apprehension about disability causes fear and can paralyse us as workers – we must overcome our fears, be prepared to take some risks, stick to our principles, adapt our methods of working to each individual child, ask for advice and use our imagination. We must not allow our own lack of expertise to place even more obstacles in the path of a disabled child having access to the quality of life every child has the right to enjoy.

Reference

1. Fahlberg V, *A Child's Journey through Placement*, BAAF, 1994.

Working with **parents**

This section could properly be placed at the beginning of the book, because working with parents comes first, whatever the aims and outcomes for the children. By leaving it until almost last, we do not mean that it is least important. We hope it is self-evident throughout the book that parents or primary carers should be closely involved in every aspect of the work: in identifying the child who needs care outside the home, in making choices about the kind of care available, and in supporting the child in the placement. But finally, the parents of children with disabilities also have a right to expect a service for themselves.

What do parents have a right to expect?

To be consulted at every stage

This principle is enshrined in the 1989 Children Act, but it is not uncommon for the parents of disabled children to complain that nobody listens to them or hears what they really say. If they ask for a sitting service so that they can go out one evening a week, they do not want to be persuaded to use respite care instead. Their cries for help may be misunderstood as signals of rejection; their reasonable requests, when they care for a very demanding child, may be interpreted as coming from aggressive, rather than advocating parents.

It may be the case that the parents' interests conflict with what is perceived to be the child's interests. If the parents believe that they have been heard and that their opinions have been taken into account, there can be negotiation, reconciliation and progress; if the parents feel their voice is ignored, their discontent will lead to stalemate and eventual conflict.[1]

When children are placed in alternative care, parents who already feel overwhelmed can easily be made to feel irrelevant. They may then limit or cut off contact, in the mistaken belief that their child needs only people more expert than themselves. In order to make a continuing contribution to their disabled children's lives, even if permanently separated from them, parents have to feel that their efforts and strengths, as well as their frailties, have been noted and appreciated. If the parents of children with disabilities feel anger, guilt, sorrow and a sense of loss about both the impairment and the separation, then they have a right not to be disarmed, but to have their pain and frustrations acknowledged. Parents will more readily share their true feelings with workers who understand their child's disability and have experience of alternative care for disabled children.

Family Group Conferences[2] may be one way to ensure that parents and relatives are given the opportunity and support to plan for a child who cannot remain permanently at home. This is still a relatively new process in the UK; it is being pioneered by the Family Rights Group and could suitably become standard procedure for children with disabilities.

Information and explanation

Parents have a right to be enabled to make informed choices.

- They need to know how to balance the advantages and drawbacks of one kind of placement against another for a child with a specific disability.
- They have to know something about likely outcomes from available research.
- They should be aware of their own rights, responsibilities and legal position in relation to the whole range of placements.
- They must be given details, preferably in writing, of the service offered and the processes involved.
- They should have access to expert guidance regarding their child's special needs, which must include consideration of ethnicity, culture, religion, education, personality and disposition, as well as disability.

After the first three months in post, I still felt I had not made the required shift in thinking and awareness towards disability services, so I decided to visit schools, parents' groups and individual parents to help me.

I initially discovered the advantages of contact with parents during a visit to foster carers who have a disabled child of their own.

22 May 95 Visit to Sandra who is a foster carer with a house which has been adapted to the needs of their severely disabled son. Useful on a number of counts:
– seeing another adapted property;
– talking through issues arising because of their particular position as parents with a severely disabled child of their own, and as foster carers offering a variety of placements. They have a special understanding of the pressures on parents because of their first-hand experience.
– having a parent's view about the services available to them. In particular, Sandra commented they would have jumped at the idea of shared care within a family setting rather than residential, which is what they were offered.

13 June 95 Visit to Brian and Jean, parents of Jessie, a 14-year-old girl who has profound learning disabilities. They belong to a group of parents of children and young people who use the residential unit for respite. A remarkable couple who have suffered many losses and these have taken their toll. But they remain stoical and positive. In addition to living with severe disability, they lost another child as a baby, and their adult daughter recently contracted a potentially fatal disease. Thankfully, she has recovered and the whole family seems to have a very positive attitude to life, often seeing the funny side of things. In talking about bringing up a severely disabled child and the services they received, or could have used, if they had been available, they conveyed very clearly to me some of the dilemmas parents face. They welcomed respite care, but although a number of family placements were tried, none of them could adequately manage Jessie's challenging behaviour. Brian and Jean thought it was better to settle for the residential unit rather than put Jessie through any more attempts at family placement with all the disruption and upset involved. They have increased the number of times they use this facility, in order to survive, but have very mixed feelings about it. They know Jessie doesn't like going – she expresses this by her behaviour – but they also know they could not manage to continue to care for her without breaks. They feel they have had to "harden their hearts" and almost ignore Jessie's feelings in this. They worry about the future and what will be available when Jessie is an adult. They know that even if they find something acceptable when the time comes, there is no guarantee of that particular provision always being there – nothing is permanent.

The only direct work I have done with individual parents has been with Peter and Rosie's parents, during the recruitment of shared care families.

15 June 95 Joint visit with social worker to Julia, mother of Peter, the 12-year-old boy with Down's Syndrome referred to me for a shared care family. The purpose of the visit was to find out about Peter's background, have another opportunity to meet a parent of a disabled child, and clarify my role (and its limitations in terms of finding families). It was helpful to meet with her and talk about Peter, his needs and her view of things.

I enjoyed meeting Julia and said I would keep in touch to let her know any progress I make in establishing a scheme for shared care. The probable wait did not seem to bother her; Peter has only recently moved to his current respite residential unit and is well settled for the time being.

6 October 95 Further visit to Julia to tell her that the proposal to pilot a shared care scheme has definitely been approved so that we can proceed to look for a shared carer for Peter. I explained about the process and that I would like us to write a pen-picture of Peter together.

23 October 95 Brief visit to Julia to show her the final version of the pen-picture we are using in the publicity. Went over what would be happening. Assured her we would keep her informed. Had some discussion about whether she should attend the Information Meeting, but we agreed that this was not appropriate and that she would not need to be involved directly until we have a particular family in mind.

- They need to understand something about people who come forward to offer alternative care to children with disabilities i.e. single parents who can devote more time to a child.
- They should be informed about the kind of residential provision available – small group home or specialist care – and the qualifications, skills and experience of staff.

Ayesha was a two-week-old baby with Down's Syndrome. Her distraught unmarried parents were students from Bangladesh who could not contemplate caring for Ayesha or taking her home to their country after they completed their studies. They were prepared to make a financial commitment but did not wish for any future direct or indirect contact. When adoption was mentioned, they were adamant that they wanted Ayesha to be brought up in a residential home with other children like herself. They insisted that their religion would not allow Ayesha to be adopted.

Ayesha was accommodated by the local authority and placed with short-term foster carers from the same ethnic background as the parents. It was made clear to the parents that no decision could be made about Ayesha's future until they were fully acquainted with the child care procedures in this country, and with the implications of various courses for Ayesha's progress and development. With the help of the foster carers and the social worker, the parents met other families with children who were looked after by the local authority. They were introduced to children with Down's Syndrome who had been adopted and to some older children with Down's Syndrome living in a small group home. They gradually took on responsibility for planning Ayesha's future; they joined MENCAP and read extensively about Down's Syndrome and alternative care.

When Ayesha was four months old, the parents agreed that she should be placed permanently with an older Bangladeshi family, who had been approved by a voluntary agency as long-term carers for a child with disabilities. This family had been recommended by the first foster carers.

Ayesha was introduced and moved in a co-operative venture by the three families concerned.

Adoption remains a vexed issue: the concept is alien to all three families, while the local authority regards it as the best way to offer permanence to Ayesha and independence to the carers. The parents do not rule out adoption if the religious question can be satisfactorily settled; there are precedents and the matter is being further explored. In the meantime, the parents feel that Ayesha is secure in her new family and making progress beyond their hopes and expectations. They have returned to Bangladesh and are keeping in touch with the local authority and with Ayesha's new family.

Information made all the difference to Ayesha's life. Without it, she could have grown up in a series of unsuitable settings, become the subject of litigation and she could have been completely severed from her roots. Her parents admit that they were at first alarmed that the local authority wanted to deny Ayesha institutional care, which they thought superior, in favour of family care, which they suspected was a poor alternative. They were also dubious about finding families who wanted children with disabilities, and immobilised by their own ignorance and fear of disability. They described the experience of learning to plan for Ayesha as a revelation.

It is, of course, possible that good information can lead to other outcomes, including appropriate residential care; certainly information should not be given as a means of persuasion. That would be poor information, and poor information leads to poor decisions.

Assessments, reviews and child care plans

The parents of disabled children have a right to have a decent assessment of their whole family's needs. They should not have to resort to special pleading in order to qualify for any particular service. A comprehensive evaluation should consider the other children in the family as well as the parents and the disabled child.

This is because we thought we might get into too much detail at an early stage if Julia were there. If there is a choice involved, I shall use her experience to help us choose, but it is more suitable for a family to hear the details of Peter's care later on.

19 October 95 Joint visit with Maureen (Rosie's social worker) to Rosie's family to discuss the project to look for a shared care family. Immediately struck by the contrast with Peter's family – opposite ends of the social spectrum. They live in a large house in a small rural town, as compared to a small flat on a council estate in a large city. The amount of space available, both indoors and out, must make a difference to a family's ability to cope with the constant demands. Met Rosie who is a very definite and, I thought, delightful character. She was in her wheelchair and sat beside me and I introduced myself – although she has no words, she made sounds and was obviously responding to me as a new person. When she smiled her whole face lit up and I had a sense of a very warm and fun-loving girl. Her father then got her up to "walk" her around for a while because it is important to keep her moving as much as possible. This task is getting more difficult as she gets bigger and may soon be impossible for one person. One of the things which became clear as we talked about Rosie was that it really needs two people to manage her most of the time.

This will obviously have major implications for any shared care arrangement. The family all chipped in to tell me about her so that we could design a pen-picture for the publicity. I explained the process and possible timescales. They were happy about it and realised we're working with the unknown as there hasn't been a shared care scheme set up here before. I think – and I warned them – that the greatest stumbling block may be the geographical limitations required in Rosie's case. I said I would work on the pen-picture following this visit and send them my ideas for comment.

1 March 96 Attended Rosie's Review (held at the family home). Let them know that we had not been successful in the first attempt to find a shared care family. This is quite depressing for everybody because the situation is becoming less and less manageable at home. There is a local residential unit which can offer a reasonable amount of respite to the family and plans for this are proceeding. We agreed to continue the search, although there a number of questions to sort out with the parents first eg. should we use Rosie's real name if we are going to use the local press. They also expressed concern about the assessment and approval procedure if we are inviting applications from the general public. We need to get together to thrash these matters out before the next attempt to recruit a family.

In fact, we have still not met to take this further. We had two meetings set up which the mother cancelled. I have left it up to the social worker to initiate any further contact about recruiting a shared care family.

In addition to these individual contacts with parents, I found my visits to groups of parents very helpful in building my understanding of disability issues.

12 June 95 Gave a talk to a group of deaf people at the Deaf Centre about adoption and fostering services. Had tried to get hold of a video on the subject but it didn't arrive on time. Will give it to them to look at later. I found it a fascinating experience. Realise I am very lacking in "deaf awareness" - eg. did not even know that a "minicom" (a text telephone) was a device linked to a telephone to enable deaf people to communicate in writing. The most interesting (and useful) part of the session was when questions raised several matters for discussion. Do agencies encourage deaf people to adopt? If so, can they only adopt a deaf child or would they be allowed to

adopt a hearing child? Is it better for a deaf child to be brought up by deaf parents? (my question to them). Could a deaf person be a foster carer? How can deaf people get information about adoption and fostering?

By the end of the afternoon I had far more questions than I could answer, but felt very challenged and stimulated by contact with this group. Clearly many of the issues are akin to those of "race" with which I am so much more familiar. Certainly deaf people have a separate culture and history of oppression, and many would not identify themselves as disabled. Need to learn more.

The resulting package could include day care, play schemes, holidays, sitting services, as well as the range of alternative care outside the home.

A receptive and sensitive approach to ethnicity, culture and religion will help to produce a well-balanced assessment. It is dangerous to make assumptions like: "all Jews look after their own" or "all Asian families feel shame about disability".[3] Parents from minority ethnic groups who have children with disabilities have the right to be assessed as a family which is trying to cope in its own unique way.

Assessments cannot be written on tablets of stone. Their value to families lies in their flexibility and responsiveness to changing situations; regular reviews are as important as the original assessment.

Parents have a right to be given copies of their assessment and of any subsequent child care plans made by the local authority. It should go without saying that assessments, reviews and child care plans work better if the parents are partners in the process.

Partnership

Parents have a right to work in partnership with the local authority and other agencies offering a service to children with disabilities and their families. If parents ask for help, it does not mean that they have nothing to contribute, and parents are usually experts in their child's specific disability.[4] They may not always make the best decisions, but neither do social workers – perhaps there is a better chance if the two heads are put together.

Even if there are prescriptive court orders, parents have unique knowledge and must be consulted about how to make the law work in the best interests of their child. It is hard for both parties to co-operate if there is a conflict; it is harder still for a social worker, who has had the unenviable duty of removing an abused or neglected child with disabilities from home, to treat the parents as equal partners in making a care plan, or for the parents to have confidence in a worker who is not a disability specialist. In such circumstances, it may be more helpful to

appoint a new worker from a disability team who can refocus the work on the child's and the family's special needs and strengths. Otherwise there is a danger that the letter of the law will be observed, but that the spirit of it will be defied.

Ian was a twelve-year-old boy with hydro-cephaly and learning difficulties, who lived with a permanent foster carer and her large family of adopted, fostered and birth children, including two others with disabilities. Ian was placed on a care order when he was ten because he had been physically abused by his step-father; his mother had failed to protect him and was deemed incapable of protecting him in the future. She did not oppose the care order, but applied for a contact order because she was apprehensive about the local authority's intentions. She agreed to monthly, supervised contact; the time and place to be at the social worker's discretion.

Ian was well placed and the mother appreciated the foster carer's commitment and Ian's evident improvement. But after a time, she complained to the court that contact was always arranged or changed at short notice, for times and days convenient to the social worker, at unsuitable venues for Ian and with a string of disapproving supervisors who knew nothing of Ian's disability. The social worker testified that Ian's mother was unreliable about visits, unpunctual when she turned up, unco-operative with the supervisors, and unstimulating for Ian. He insisted that Ian would again be at risk from the step-father if contact were to be unsupervised. The foster carer stated that Ian wanted to see his mother and was unable to understand if anything went wrong. She believed that the mother wished to keep Ian safe in the foster home and would not try to take him home. The Judge ordered that contact should continue to be monthly and supervised, but that the social worker should give at least two weeks notice in writing of each visit, which should always take place on a Monday or Thursday, the mother's days off work, at a place with provision for children with disabilities and supervised by someone who knew the case.

10 May 95 Attended a meeting of the Down's Parents and Toddlers Group at the Hospital Child Development Centre. Busy, active, lively group – positive atmosphere. Parents are encouraged to come along from early on in their child's life. There was good interaction between the children and the adults seemed to feel at home and at ease with each other. One Asian family was there for the first time and was made very welcome. They were asking the other parents a lot of questions, particularly about their children's development. They were quite surprised by the general level of mobility and other skills of the children there. This seemed to be a helpful step for them in understanding the diagnosis and what it might mean for their child. But there were no other Asian families there today, so I wonder if they will feel it is really a "white group" …

Chatted with some of the parents and had the general impression that the service from the Child Development Centre was appreciated, particularly this group which provides opportunities to meet with other parents and the professional staff on a regular basis. One of the mothers has adopted two babies with Down's Syndrome through Barnardo's. She seemed to be at ease, and accepted by the group. I sat for a while with her and one of the other mothers, and it was obvious that they had talked about the differences inherent in giving birth to a child with Down's Syndrome and all the adjustments needed in that situation, and choosing to adopt. This appears to be a supportive group for birth as well as adoptive parents.

20 June 95 Visit to the Asian mothers' group which meets at the residential respite unit for profoundly disabled children. A very animated and friendly gathering. Some of the women spoke English and translated for the other women. I told them about my post and its purpose and they told me about the history of their group. Originally social workers were involved but now they are a self-help group. They prefer it without the social workers running it. They got some help from an organisation based in Leeds – Contact a Parent – and they now function very successfully. They all use the family placement scheme for respite during the day, but were adamant that it would be unacceptable within their families and their wider community to use another family to care for their children overnight. So, for any substantial respite care, they use the residential unit.

I'm puzzled by this because I understood from the workers on the family respite scheme that Asian families use it frequently – I'll need to check this. The group meets once a week and they have a creche run by a volunteer, so they can make the most of discussions but the meetings often take the form of social events and outings.

28 June 95 Attended another of the parents' support groups at the Child Development Centre. This group has been meeting for years, starting when the children were pre-school, and they are all now in their teens or early twenties. Mostly I just listened, because the main reason for my visit was to get to know about the dilemmas facing parents of disabled young adults. They regard this group as one of their mainstays because of the unique support they have given each other throughout the years. Most problems seem to be practical – finding out how to get the right kind of equipment to suit their particular child's needs, having accurate information about services and state benefits – but also finding the emotional and physical strength to go on despite huge setbacks, constant demands, and, very commonly, exhaustion. Professionals who listened to them were valued.

We discussed ideas I have been formulating about shared care, which met with mixed feelings. Some felt it would be very difficult, if not impossible, to find families who could cope. They also spoke of the risk of abuse within a foster home, sensing that their children were particularly vulnerable. Some felt "beholden" to respite families who were doing it as volunteers, and felt they always had to fit in with what suited the respite family, rather than having a service when they needed it. There was also some talk about the stigma of fostering as opposed to respite care – if your child went into foster care it meant you were a bad parent, whereas respite care is seen as a service.

2 February 96 Attended Day Conference on autism. Luckily found myself in the same small discussion group as two of our parents. Spent lunch-time with them and other parents. Started a useful dialogue about shared care and their perception of fostering. They echoed strongly the opinions of the other group of parents I had met at the Child Development Centre. They also have regular meetings and would be happy for me to attend one of them, so I shall arrange to do that soon.

The social worker, who was a member of the child protection unit, complied precisely with the directions. He found a family centre with a soft environment and play materials; he meticulously arranged dates and times via curt notes two weeks ahead, on the days stipulated; and he now supervised the meetings himself. When the mother applied for an extra contact visit on Ian's twelfth birthday, she was turned down because neither the family centre nor the social worker were available.

The mother became increasingly dissatisfied without being able to formulate why. Finally she contacted a worker in the disability team who had visited the family before the abuse proceedings, and had known Ian since he was five. This worker agreed with the child protection unit that she would take over the supervision and arranging of contact. Nothing changed, but immediately everything felt different. The monthly contact visits were preceded by discussions about Ian's needs and medical condition and followed up with a shared feedback about the meeting and Ian's progress. The worker encouraged the mother in her efforts to engage with Ian who easily withdrew into his private world but now began to be more responsive. The mother felt validated as a good parent and regained her confidence in handling Ian.

In due course, the mother was invited to go with the foster carer when she took Ian for regular check-ups to the hospital, to attend school functions, and to join the foster family for special occasions and celebrations. She has accepted that she must take responsibility for keeping her husband away from Ian and has made no attempt to include him in contact arrangements. Her understanding of her son's disability is proving invaluable to the foster carer.

When true partnership was offered, Ian's mother was able to become an active, reliable parent and consequently was no longer regarded as troublesome by the child protection team. Parents as partners can offer continuity and hard won expertise to their disabled children, and they can be a valuable resource for any agency which works with them. Why, we have to wonder, would anyone want to turn parents into clients when they can be partners?

Even when adoption transfers the legal parental responsibility, most birth parents continue to have a contribution to make. Parents, we have learned, remain parents for life.

Support

Parents of children with disabilities have a right to expect maximum support, including financial support, to keep their children at home full time, part time or not at all. It can be as painful to hold on as it is to let go. Families have to find out for themselves what they can and what they cannot manage to do; how much support they can use and from where it would be welcome. Relatives, friends and neighbours are the most natural source of support, but social workers must be ready to fill the gaps.

Tim and Mark were five-year-old twins. Tim was severely brain damaged at birth; he had no speech, could not walk or feed himself. He babbled cheerfully and was very affectionate. Mark was a bright competent little boy. He made friends easily and was fiercely protective of Tim. There were two other children in the family: a girl of ten and a girl of twelve, both doing well at school and leading a busy social life. The parents were calm and capable and took each day with Tim as it came. They asked for help when they needed it, and used respite care in the school holidays so that they could get away and concentrate on the other children.

The family pattern changed when Mark started school. The mother went back to college part time to finish a degree course interrupted by the twins' birth, the father developed diabetes, and Tim's condition deteriorated – he needed almost constant attention and frequent hospitalisation. The parents sadly agreed that they could no longer look after Tim without damaging their own health and putting their other children's welfare at risk.

19 March 96 Attended meeting of the parents of children with autism. Another long-standing group that offers consistent support and seems very welcoming to newer members. I described my job and they talked about their concerns. Finding resources that are geared specifically enough to their children's needs is one of the greatest difficulties. Services geared primarily to children with learning disabilities are not necessarily appropriate. Residential units for respite are one example, and these parents felt that highly specialised provision was needed because of the very different behaviour and particular set of problems that autism seems to bring. It was obvious to me that one of the benefits of this group, apart from mutual support, is its ability to act as a pressure group. I pursued the possibility of developing shared family care, and they had doubts about its feasibility for children with autism. But, on the other hand, they did feel that individualised care would be greatly preferable to group care. They were interested to hear about the success of the Leeds scheme (Section Two), which includes children with autism, and were open-minded, if cautious, about our project.

16 April 96 One other piece of work I undertook recently involved some direct counselling of parents shortly after their child's birth. I was asked by the duty officer to advise who could offer specialised counselling to parents who had just given birth to a baby with Down's Syndrome. They are, apparently, rejecting the baby and asking for adoption. I suggested contacting the Children with Disabilities Team as I imagine they may often offer counselling of this sort to parents.

17 April 96 Overheard one of the disability workers commenting to another that she had been approached by the fostering unit about counselling these parents but had referred it back to the fostering unit. I joined in the conversation, explaining I had initiated the contact with their team because I thought they would have the relevant expertise. The disability social workers felt it was inappropriate for them to get involved, because, since the parents were requesting adoption at this stage, it might feel like pressure to keep the child if a disability specialist offered them counselling. I could see the point, but wondered if there was any routine counselling of parents giving birth to a disabled child. No, this would be an impossible task considering the numbers involved – also, they both felt completely unskilled in the area of relinquishing a child for adoption. This is simply not something which crops up in their work. To the best of their knowledge, parents of disabled children do not, nowadays, consider the option of not retaining responsibility for their child. So I agreed it was an inappropriate referral for them.

It would make sense for me to offer a time-limited piece of work to these parents, given my knowledge of adoption, and some growing knowledge of disability.

Later, telephoned the area social worker dealing with this case and offered to counsel the parents. Arranged a joint interview with her next week.

23 April 96 Joint visit to Ann and David at home. Explained my role and asked how they were feeling about the baby now. They are still very upset but not suffering from the acute shock they experienced on discovering their son's diagnosis. They have visited him twice in the foster home, and have explained to their three-year-old son that the baby is "poorly" and so has to be looked after by special people. They did take him to see his brother and he held him (although the baby did not really wake up on that visit). They had originally been going to tell him that the baby had died, but on reflection realised that would not be right. They seem to have good support from family and friends, and are allowing themselves to express whatever feelings they are experiencing. They are undecided about the future for their baby, and want to use the next few weeks to find out as much as possible about Down's Syndrome.

They were also keen to hear about the process of adoption and I told them how adoption has changed, and that it would not mean the baby disappears from their life forever. I talked about the practicalities of the letter-box system, providing at least annual information both ways, and I also touched on the emotional issues involved; the ongoing feeling of loss for them and the fact that adoption would not get rid of the pain they are currently feeling. They seem very receptive, and are quite relieved that there is this element of openness in adoption these days.

They are meeting with the specialist health visitor this week and have also set up a visit from a parent of a toddler with Down's Syndrome. They have managed to find some reading material, but asked if I could recommend more for them, both on the subject of adoption and about Down's Syndrome, which I agreed to do.

They had read about the possibility of adoption for children with severe disabilities and they had heard about "open adoptions" from a social worker friend. They now approached their local authority with a request to arrange an "open adoption" for Tim. The family placement worker was entirely discouraging. She said it would take a small miracle to find any adopters for Tim and that any mention of contact, let alone "open adoption", would put everybody off. She was also disapproving of a family who, as she saw it, cold-bloodedly rejected their child on the one hand, but wanted to have their cake and eat it on the other.

The parents persevered. They explained that it had been a traumatic decision to reach; they felt strongly that Tim needed a family without other young children; they were not trying to hang on but felt equally strongly that they had a continuing contribution to make to Tim's life. They persuaded the local authority to allow them to design the publicity to recruit a family for Tim.

The parents wrote the publicity in the form of an open letter which was published in various disability newsletters. In the letter, they described Tim's life so far, their reasons for choosing adoption, their view of Tim's needs, and their hopes for continuity.

The publicity produced Ruth, a single woman who had taken very early retirement when the children's home, where she was assistant matron, closed down. Ruth adopted Tim and has always looked upon his birth family as a bonus. Mark regularly comes to stay and the older girls visit occasionally. The birth parents also visit, and are available at any time if Ruth wants information about the past or to talk over any new developments. But there is never any doubt about who is in charge: Ruth is Tim's legal, practical and psychological mother.

Not all families are as strong and decisive as the one in the case above. Tim's parents were able to take the lead in assessing their own capacities and needs and to ask for support as and if they wanted it. When it wasn't forthcoming, they were confident enough to make innovative plans without it. Most parents, however, will require support as they move from one stage to another with their child, even if they have clear ideas of what the next stage should be and how to achieve it:

- support to see respite care and other forms of shared care as positive;
- support to keep the child in the family;
- support to place the child in appropriate alternative care if necessary;
- support to maintain contact and remain involved.

Working in partnership with parents and giving them support are not mutually exclusive. Hearing what parents say and giving information should go hand in hand. A comprehensive service for families who have children with disabilities should enable the parents to look after their children, whether they are at home or in alternative care, but it should also enable them to look after themselves and the rest of their family.

References

1. Hare P, *Listening to Parents: Support services for families of children who have special needs – A survey of parents' views*, NCH Action for Children, 1992.
2. Tunnard J, *Family Group Conferences*, Family Rights Group, 1994.
3. Shah R, *The Silent Minority: Children with disabilities in Asian families*, National Children's Bureau, 1992.
4. Russell P, *Positive Choices: Services for children with disabilities living away from home*, Council for Disabled Children, 1996.

The social worker from the Area then made some arrangements with them about contact with the baby, and an Accommodation Meeting. We both stressed that they had plenty of time to make decisions and that there would be no pressure on them. Arranged to visit on my own next week.

30 April 96 Visit to Ann and David. They seemed more composed, and spoke about the contact they had had with the baby which had gone well. He was more wakeful and responsive, and they were planning to see the heart specialist with him next week. They found the visits from both the Health Visitor and the parent of the Down's Syndrome toddler helpful in giving them a realistic picture of what life might be like if they decide to keep the baby. I gave them the various books I had brought for them to look at, and talked with them again about adoption and what it would involve. They asked lots of questions and it certainly looks as if this is the direction of their thinking still. They have enquired about education and found out that in the early years the child could be taught in a mainstream school, but probably not at secondary level.

I asked them what the main block was to caring for this child themselves, and I was surprised when Ann answered that it was primarily the extra work involved in looking after a disabled child, which she felt she would not be capable of. There was also the impact on their older child because of the amount of time and attention this child would require. I think I was expecting

something about the stigma, or the long-term worries. Emphasised the need to give themselves space and time to make a decision, and arranged to see them again in two weeks.

14 May 96 Saw Ann and David again. They immediately said that they felt sure that they wanted to place their son for adoption and that they felt comfortable with this decision. They have continued to visit him on a weekly basis and show much parental care and interest. They simply do not feel equipped to bring him up and feel that another family would do a better job. We went through what happens next and how long it might take. This was a fairly brief session. I suggested that they try to write down as much as possible of their experience of the last few weeks, because this would be very helpful for any adoptive parents, to explain why their baby could not grow up in his birth family. We also talked about them meeting and being involved in any choice of adoptive parents. I suggested they might wish to give him something to take with him throughout his life. They would like to do this, but the idea of it made Ann tearful.

They are going away on holiday for a week and they said they would use the opportunity to review their decision to be sure it was the right one. I said I would contact them on their return.

15 May 96 Memo to Senior Care Manager to let her know about this baby and that we would be needing to identify an adoptive family.

Ann and David have confirmed their wish to place their baby for adoption and so the work is now being undertaken in the usual way ie. the Area social worker is working with the parents and child while the worker in the Adoption and Fostering Unit will be finding a placement and liaising closely with the Area worker. I think this has been a good example of how a specialist post such as mine can be used.

One aspect of this case which interests me is the lack of expertise within the specialist disability team in counselling parents who wish to relinquish care of their children. I wonder if the culture of keeping your disabled child and coping, despite all problems, has led to a situation where it is unacceptable for parents (and

workers?) to contemplate choosing not to. Of course this is preferable to the culture, prevalent not so long ago, when parents were advised not to take their severely disabled children home from hospital, and whole generations of disabled people grew up in the large institutions for "handicapped people". However, parents who wish to consider alternative care must be allowed and supported to do so. The whole range of placements should be available to them, including the option of sharing with others the care of their disabled children. If we succeed in maintaining disabled children within their own families through developing shared care arrangements, perhaps we can lead the way to similar initiatives for non-disabled children.

Postscript: when things don't work out

Although common sense, good practice and the 1989 Children Act dictate that 'disabled children need accommodation not unsuitable to their disability', the right provision is not always available. Financial constraints force rationing, foster care and adoptive placements of children with disabilities do disrupt, parents under stress who may be sharing their disabled child's care can become embroiled in family problems or even breakdown, and residential homes close down. Text books do not reproduce the daily reality of social services, as evidenced by the diary in this one.

Unforeseen as well as unforeseeable circumstances can make the best laid plans go awry. Understandably, children with disabilities may then be placed wherever there is a vacancy, but unless parents or social workers are very determined, they may remain in the wrong place for the wrong reasons for a long time. If a carefully chosen placement does not work out, it is easy to become disheartened about finding and assessing another.

Giving information, offering support and hearing what people say, which have been recurring themes throughout this book, will not have been wasted if there is a disruption of a placement, a failed introduction or an unachieved plan. On the contrary, it is crucial that an exchange of information, support for all concerned, and listening to each other continue, so that parents, agency and carers can work together to make a better placement next time. We learn as much from plans and placements which do not work as we do from those which do, although it is a painful process and one which we would all prefer not to endure.

It is bad enough when any child is rejected, for whatever reason; if the child has a disability, everyone will feel worse about it. If a placement was never made, parents may see their child's impairment as the reason for not finding one,

and the whole family could suffer from a sense of failure. Social workers can become immobilised by the fear that further work could do further harm, thus adding to the difficulties faced by the child. And prospective carers, who with preparation and good will could not fulfil a promise or an intention, may believe that they have nothing other than guilt to contribute to any future plan.

Disruption or failure to find the right placement are no-one's fault. Everyone always wants it to work for the child and suffers when it does not. If mistakes are made, they are not made deliberately; if the right placement has not been found, perhaps a reassessment of needs is required; if a placement disrupts, perhaps something unpredictable occurred.

Clare moved to a well prepared family from a home for children with disabilities – where she had lived almost since birth – when she was nine years old. The family expected the withdrawn behaviour, the epileptic fits, the learning difficulties and the speech impairment. They had spent hours with her residential workers and her teachers; they had met her mother who lived in a different part of the country and agreed to keep in touch with her. They had learned all they could about her particular disabilities from the agency medical adviser and Clare's paediatrician. They had an older disabled daughter by birth and belonged to a network of parents of children with disabilities. They were committed to Clare and had every intention of making her a permanent member of their family.

Unfortunately, no-one had warned them about Clare's habit of wandering around the house, emptying out every drawer and cupboard she could find and then carefully putting the contents back in the wrong places. This behaviour had apparently not disturbed anyone in the residential home, where the children's personal belongings had not been valued and where access to kitchen, bathroom and staff rooms was not allowed; it was even seen as something which gave Clare harmless enjoyment and left the staff free to cope with more troublesome children. For the new family it was the worst scenario. The mother spent all day looking for cutlery among her underwear and rescuing documents from the linen cupboard. The father, an accountant who worked partly from home, had to lock away every piece of paper and office equipment. The older daughter of the family became upset because all her toys and clothes were messed up and sometimes torn or broken.

The more the family tried to stop or to distract Clare from her obsessive occupation, the more determined and secretive Clare became about her business. After one particularly trying day, when the carers thought they had finally managed to persuade Clare to restrict herself to her own drawers, Clare got up in the middle of the night to perform her dreadful deeds.

Every reader will by now have some solution in mind; it should indeed have been possible to help the family to devise a step-by-step programme to curb Clare's unacceptable behaviour. But the unforeseen circumstance in this placement was not solely Clare's habit of taking everything out of drawers, it was also the family's need for order. The parents had made tremendous emotional and psychological adjustments when their daughter was born and they went on adjusting as time went by. They rightly saw themselves and were seen as a flexible couple, but they had a sticking point: they had to keep control of the material things in life to counterbalance that flexibility. They could no more have verbalised this need, or foreseen its relevance to Clare's placement with them, than the residential workers could visualise the shattering effect, of what they regarded as Clare's unremarkable behaviour, on a family. And the placement worker could not possibly have prepared the family or the child for such an unpredictable situation. The placement disrupted after six weeks.

Peter: The placement of Peter with Jackie and Ian was approved by the Fostering Panel on 24 May '96 but is being delayed until alterations are made to the house as recommended by the Occupational Therapist – more substantial than any of us had anticipated. Peter is spending three days a week with Jackie, but sleeping at the respite unit – he has adapted to this more easily than we expected. The time he spends with Jackie is going very well and we are all impatient for it to include overnight stays. Peter's mother, Julia, is working closely with Jackie.

Andrew and Gary: The family who came forward for Andrew has withdrawn. No reason given. Discussions between managers in the two Divisions have proceeded and there is a plan to look at opening a small residential unit for disabled children who need full-time care. Andrew and Gary would be placed there while plans for recruiting families proceed.

Rosie: Rosie is using the local residential respite unit despite some settling in problems. Her parents would still prefer a family to share the care.

Rebecca: Rebecca's care is being shared by her father and the foster carers as arranged. There has been no diminishing of his involvement or commitment. Eventual rehabilitation is still the aim but is becoming less likely.

Organisational developments

The Department has decided to create a permanent post to continue the work initiated in this trial period. One of the tasks will be developing the Shared Care scheme. There are now ten children referred for shared care. The Adoption and Fostering Unit reviewed its preparation process and introduced a core series of preparation groups relevant to all carers. This should cut down the lengthy waits some prospective carers had to endure previously.

Following the departure of the Assistant Director of the Disability and Community Health Division, there was a lengthy debate within the Department regarding the future of that Division. There were strong lobbies both to retain the Division and to merge with other services. Finally, because of a strong political view, the decision was made to retain the Disability Division. Strategic planning for disabled children within the "looked-after" system will continue to present a major challenge and should be addressed within the Children's Services Plan currently being formulated. There is still a real danger of disabled children and their carers being left on the margins of both sides of the service. The holder of the new specialist foster care post will have to forge and maintain strong links between the two Divisions if disabled children are to get the best of both worlds.

Only when the family, the placement worker and the residential workers met to explore exactly what had gone wrong and why, did the full impact of Clare's behaviour on the family's defence system emerge. It was then easy to decide that Clare's habits could and should be changed in the residential home with the help of a therapist, in preparation for a future family placement. There was a chance that she would regress when she moved again, but the next prospective adopters would be aware of that and be ready to cope. When the family realised that their views were valued and that they were not blamed for the disruption, they were able to say what a lovely girl Clare was and to show how upset they felt about losing her.

Clare did not fully understand why she had to go back to the children's home or why she had left it in the first place; she gladly accepted the extra attention she was given, the continuing contact with the family who could not manage, and their promise that they would help to find her another family which could. So far, "family" had meant no more to Clare than having a long lasting treat. Her preoccupation with drawers receded when the play therapist opened up the recesses of Clare's life story – work which had been previously attempted but had clearly not got through to Clare. The staff in the residential home backed up the therapist's work with a behaviour modification programme, so that the habit as well as the obsession were tackled. It was a slow process, with several set-backs, but a year later Clare was successfully placed with a family.

Getting together and trying to understand what has or has not happened can create the enthusiasm and energy to proceed to the next stage, armed with new knowledge and insights. Managing disruptions and the techniques of disruption meetings are fully covered in two guides published by BAAF.[1,2] The disability factor is just one more aspect to take into account if plans go awry – and some of them inevitably will. It is not possible to get it right every time when children, parents, present and prospective carers and a variety of social workers have to mix and try to match their experiences, attitudes and expectations of complex matters such as patterns of child care, family systems, rights and responsibilities, contact and continuity, ethnicity, culture and religion, and disability. It is remarkable and a tribute to all concerned that it so often does work.

References

1. Fitzgerald J, *Understanding Disruption*, BAAF, 1990.
2. Smith S, *Learning from Disruption: Making better placements*, BAAF, 1994.

Appendix A
Adoption information

This list has been compiled for all adoptions. It may have to be adjusted if the child has disabilities, but the disability should never be used as a reason to withhold or disregard information.

For the child

a) Photographs of birth family, carers and previous homes.
b) Life story record appropriate to understanding.
c) An address book, or equivalent, with names, addresses and telephone numbers of significant people in child's life.
d) A diary or equivalent with details of contact arrangements including letter box service if applicable.
e) A letter/video/cassette from the birth family telling their own story and, where possible, giving permission for the child to have a new family.
f) Medical information about the birth parents including genetic familial disorders (to be given to adopters before placement).
g) Printed information about an adopted person's right to access to birth records when aged 18 (to be held by adopters).
h) Printed information about the Contact Register (to be held by adopters).
i) A background letter giving full information about everything known of the child's history and birth family at the time of placement, including full details of ethnic, cultural, religious and linguistic heritage (this is a statutory obligation under the Adoption Agency Regulations).
j) Family tree, keepsakes, maps, etc.

For the parents

a) A written explanation about the meaning and process of adoption and birth parents' rights.
b) A written statement of agency policy and practice regarding adoption including details of services available.
c) Written notification of adoption panel decisions.
d) A written, if necessary unidentifying, profile of the adopting family, with photographs whenever possible.
e) A copy of the contact agreement including clear explanation of letterbox service if applicable.
f) Printed information about the Contact Register.
g) Printed information about access to birth records.
h) Written information about post-adoption services available to birth parents.
i) Written information about national and local self-help groups.

For the adopters

a) Written medical information about the child, copies of assessment reports plus guidance on how new information which comes to light can be shared.
b) Written background information about the child and family.
c) Written information about the legal adoption process.
d) A copy of the contact agreement including a clear explanation of letter box service if applicable.
e) Written information about the agency's adoption services including post-adoption counselling and mediation.
f) Copies of child's school reports and any educational statements.
g) Any additional information about the child known to the adoption agency.
h) Book lists about adoption/disability for adults and children.
i) Resource pack relating to child's ethnic and cultural background if this is not reflected within the adoptive family.

Appendix B
Checklist for social workers

1) Does your authority provide a comprehensive service for children with disabilities? What does that include?

2) Have child and parents been offered every support, including respite care, aids and adaptations and financial help, to keep the child at home?

3) Check your attitudes:
a) Do you really believe that this child can be appropriately placed?
b) Do you believe that parents can be partners in planning for their child; can you accept being only a partner?
c) Do you believe that attitudes to impairment are more disabling than the impairment itself?
d) Do you believe that alternative carers need more preparation than assessment?
e) Do you believe that ethnicity, religion and culture matter to children with disabilities?

4) Are you listening and can you hear the child, the parents, present, past and future carers?

5) Has everyone got all the information available? Is more required?

6) Have the child's attachments been assessed and taken into account?

7) Has the quality as well as the quantity of contact been assured?

8) If family contact is impossible or unsatisfactory, does the child need an independent visitor or befriender?

9) Do the child/family/carers receive all the benefits and allowances to which they are entitled; do you really know what all the entitlements are, and if not, who would?

10) Do the post-placement services meet all the parties' needs?

11) Has the disability factor been understood and firmly kept in mind?

12) If this was your child, would you be satisfied with the arrangements and would you feel properly respected as the parent?

Appendix C
Glossary of **disabilities** and **implications for care**

There are a great many specific conditions and rare syndromes which impair functioning and may be termed a disability. A comprehensive and very full directory is published by CaF (Contact a Family) and is available from the address listed in Appendix E. The following list is restricted to brief information about the conditions which occur most frequently and those mentioned in this book. This list has been compiled with the aid of *The CaF Directory*.

Angelman Syndrome

A neurological disorder causing severe developmental delay and speech defects, seizures and abnormal gait. Affected children tend to laugh inappropriately and to protrude their tongues; they are usually affectionate and cheerful. Many children become toilet trained and learn to feed themselves, but they will require a high level of supervision.

Ascots Syndrome

An extremely rare condition which prevents the pre-natal development of the eyelids, lips, palate, ears, nose and sex organs. Babies born with this syndrome have an alarming appearance and require extensive plastic surgery throughout childhood. There is no link with mental development or life expectancy but the facial disfigurement will be a life-long factor and may cause serious psychological problems.

Autism

This is a pervasive developmental disorder which affects social and communication skills. There may be other learning difficulties. Characteristic behaviour is obsessive and withdrawn. Children with autism can be exhausting to care for because rules, language, and social interaction are incomprehensible to them.

Brittle bone diseases

This is a group of conditions characterised by excessive fragility of the bones in childhood. Children severely affected can sustain multiple fractures on the slightest impact. They require careful handling and may have to use a wheelchair. The severity of the condition varies.

Cerebral Palsy

This condition is the result of damage to the part of the brain concerned with movement. The effects may be slight or severe and include spasticity (disordered movement control), athetosis (frequent involuntary movements) and ataxia (unsteady gait). Adjacent parts of the brain may also be affected and lead to impaired hearing and sight and to learning difficulties. Each child will present a different set of challenges.

Cystic Fibrosis

This causes the mucous glands to produce abnormally thick mucus and the sweat glands to produce excess salt. The lungs and the pancreas are the most affected. The mucus blocks the airways which are damaged by repeated infections. The channels of the pancreas also become blocked and cysts are formed leading to fibrosis of the pancreas and possibly to diabetes. Cystic fibrosis is a life threatening condition. Seventy five per cent of affected children now survive into young adulthood; the average life expectancy is almost 30 years. It is most important to avoid infections and to have regular physiotherapy, including daily exercises at home.

Deafblindness / Rubella damaged

Deafblindness may be the result of an infection such as meningitis, or it may be a congenital defect most commonly caused by Rubella during the mother's early pregnancy. Additional congenital abnormalities may be present. All deafblind children have a dual sensory deprivation ranging from partial to total; they will require specialised education and services.

Diabetes Insipidus

A rare metabolic disorder in which the child produces large quantities of dilute urine and is constantly thirsty. It is due to a hormone deficiency which is frequently associated with a growth hormone deficiency. The fluid intake and fluid loss have to be balanced day and night – a serious imbalance requires immediate hospitalisation. Medication instructions have to be meticulously observed.

Down's Syndrome

This is a congenital chromosome abnormality. Children who are affected have distinctive features and mild to severe learning difficulties. Associated conditions are eye, heart and respiratory defects. The life expectancy of children with Down's Syndrome has been greatly enhanced by the introduction of antibiotics to fight infections. They have been described by their families as 'just a different kind of normal person'.

Epilepsy

A tendency to have recurrent seizures due to an excessive or disordered discharge of brain cells. The cause may be associated with other disabling conditions or may be intrinsic to the individual's genetic make up. Seizures may be minor absences of consciousness (*petit mal*) or major and convulsive episodes with unconsciousness. Children severely affected require close monitoring and may need to wear a crash helmet to protect their heads when they fall.

Foetal Alcohol Syndrome

This Syndrome describes a pattern of physical, behavioural and intellectual characteristics that children may display if prenatally exposed to alcohol. This can include growth deficiency, a distinctive pattern of facial features and central nervous system dysfunction. There is a wide range of functioning for individuals diagnosed with this condition from severe learning difficulties to above average ability. Most will have some difficulty with processing information. These effects are permanent but most children will make some progress as they move towards adulthood.

Hydrocephalus

This is an obstruction to the natural flow of Cerebro Spinal fluid which can result in the enlargement of the head in young babies. Usually a shunt (a piece of tube with a pressure valve) is inserted to prevent the condition from worsening but some brain damage may be sustained. Shunts can become blocked and cause further damage if not checked immediately when symptoms appear. Hydrocephaly is frequently associated with spina bifida.

Microcephaly

In Microcephaly there is a defect in the growth mechanism of the brain which makes it smaller than a normal brain; consequently the head remains small in relation to the rest of the body. This can be caused by genetic disorders and abnormalities, or by pre-natal and some post-natal infections. The resulting disabilities are varied but a degree of general developmental retardation is usual. Life expectancy depends on the severity of each case and management problems depend on the disabilities presented.

Moebius Syndrome

A rare condition characterised by paralysis of the face muscles and limitations of tongue movement leading to expressionless facial features and speech defects. The syndrome is usually accompanied by short limbs, webbed fingers or toes, rib abnormalities, and sometimes, by learning difficulties. It is important for affected children to have intensive speech therapy as early as possible; impaired speech can be an obstacle to mainstream education which would otherwise be appropriate.

Muscular Dystrophy

Muscular dystrophies are a group of progressive, inherited neuromuscular disorders. Some conditions are severe and life threatening, others are milder; a few are treatable. All muscular dystrophies are characterised by a wasting of muscle fibre and the replacement of damaged muscles by other fatty tissues. Duchenne Dystrophy is nearly always restricted to boys. Affected children require help with daily care and most often use a wheelchair.

Noonan Syndrome

This a genetic condition which is very variable in degree but may include heart defects, drooping eyelids, widely spaced eyes, flat nose, some hearing loss, short neck with or without extra folds, low hairline, low set ears, short stature, undescended testicles, and mild developmental delay. Some affected children present behaviour problems which have been associated with the syndrome.

Paraplegia

Paralysis of both legs, usually accompanied by loss of sensation in the lower body, for instance, bladder function.

Quadriplegia

Paralysis of all four limbs accompanied by loss of sensation in the body.

Rett Syndrome

This syndrome affects only females and is due to a genetic defect which usually manifests itself towards the end of the first year. Between one and two years of age there is a period of regression when skills deteriorate and the child becomes withdrawn. Periods of alternative deep breathing and breath holding are common. Following the regression it is clear that the girl has severe learning difficulties and has lost whatever speech she had. She may develop weak muscles, rigid legs, foot deformities and seizures. Although many girls continue to walk, some may need to use a wheelchair; most will reach adulthood. Children with Rett Syndrome require very high levels of help and attention.

Sickle Cell Anaemia

This condition is due to an abnormality of the haemoglobin in the blood stream. It can cause painful swellings of the hands and feet, infections, anaemia and pains in the joints and abdomen. Particularly painful episodes are known as a "painful crisis" and may have been brought on by strenuous exercise, dehydration, anaesthetics or infections – all of which have implications for care. Other problems associated with Sickle Cell Anaemia are jaundice, strokes, blood in the urine, leg ulcers and delayed growth. The condition is more common in people of African Caribbean or Mediterranean origins.

Smith-Magenis Syndrome

Children with this syndrome, which is caused by a chromosome abnormality, exhibit a number of unusual physical and behavioural characteristics. Some development delay, short fingers and toes and stature, a flat face, chronic ear infections, a strange gait, decreased sensitivity to pain and difficulty in chewing may be accompanied by self injury, sleep disturbance, hyperactivity, destructive and agressive behaviour. While Smith-Magenis Syndrome is not common, it is probably underdiagnosed because the symptoms could pass for an unspecified condition of severe and multiple disabilities.

Spina Bifida

Spina Bifida occurs when the newborn baby has part of its spinal cord and coverings exposed through a gap in the backbone. The resulting disabilities may include paralysis of the legs, incontinence, and brain damage from commonly associated hydrocephalus. The extent of the damage depends on the type of spina bifida and on the site of the defect.

Thalassaemia Major

Children with this condition, caused by an abnormality in the structure of the haemoglobin in the bloodstream, appear normal at birth but become anaemic between 3–18 months. They become pale, do not sleep well and vomit feeds. If untreated, the condition is fatal, but frequent blood transfusions combined with desferal therapy (to remove iron build up from the body) allow most children to live normal healthy lives. This condition is most common among people from Asian and Mediterranean countries.

Tuberous Sclerosis

Tuberous (swellings or enlargements) Sclerosis (the hardening of an organ or tissue) is a genetic disorder which may invade many of the body systems. Typically the brain, skin, heart, eyes, kidneys bones, lungs and intestines are affected. Seizures and some degree of retardation are usual; behaviour problems and autistic tendencies are common. However, this condition is variable, and some children may never present more than one feature while others will have every possible manifestation and a short life expectancy.

Turner Syndrome

This has many similarities with the special features of Noonan Syndrome but only affects girls. At an appropriate age they have to be given oestrogen to develop secondary sexual characteristics, but they will be infertile because they do not have ovaries. Sleeping and feeding problems may occur in early childhood and these may be followed by learning and behavioural difficulties.

Undiagnosed Children

Although there has been significant progress in the diagnosis of disabilities, there are some disabled children who remain undiagnosed because the cause and prognosis of their condition cannot be established. There are some cases where severe and multiple abnormalities are present without a specific cause, and others where mild but general developmental delay has no apparent cause. It is often more difficult to deal with an unnamed disorder than one which can be labelled and explained.

Williams Syndrome

Facial features include prominent cheeks, upturned nose, wide mouth and irregular teeth. Most affected children have a heart problem. This condition is also related to psychological and behavioural problems, for instance, hyperactivity, short attention span, and obsessional traits. Peculiar to the syndrome are an increased verbal ability in comparison to other cognitive skills which may be impaired, and hypersensitivity to loud noises.

Appendix D
Further reading

Argent H, *Practice Note 34, Placement of Children with Disabilities*, BAAF, 1996.

Baldwin S and Carlisle J, *Social Support for Disabled Children and their Families*, HMSO, 1994.

Beckford V and Robinson C, *A Second Survey of Family Based Respite Care Services in the UK*, Norah Fry Research Centre, University of Bristol, 1993.

Begum N, Hill M, and Stevens A (eds), *Reflections: The views of black disabled people on their lives and community care*, CCETSW, 1994.

Beresford B, *Positively Parents: Caring for a severely disabled child*, HMSO, 1994.

Brimblecombe F and Russell P, *Honeylands: Developing a service for families with handicapped children*, NCB, 1988.

Cowen A, *Taking Care: A guide for parents and carers about provision and services for disabled children*, Joseph Rowntree Foundation for the Family Fund, 1994.

Hirst M and Baldwin S, *Unequal Opportunities: Growing up disabled*, Social Policy Research Unit, 1994.

Howe D (ed), *Attachment and Loss in Child and Family Social Work*, Avebury, 1996.

Kennedy M, 'Sexual Abuse and Disabled Children' in Morris J (ed), *Feminism and Disability*, The Women's Press, 1996.

Kupfer F, *Before and After Zachariah: A parent's story*, Gollancz, 1982.

Learoyd C, *Matthew, My Son's Struggle: An adopter's story*, Macdonald, Queen Anne Press, 1989.

Looking After Children Project, Bulletin No.4: *Concerning Disability*, Dartington Social Research Unit, 1993.

Macadam M and Robinson C, *Balancing the Act: The impact of the Children Act 1989 on family link services for children with disabilities*, NCB, 1995.

Marchant R and Page M, *Bridging the Gap: Child protection work with children with multiple disabilities*, NSPCC, 1993.

Mountney J, *Children with Disabilities in Foster Care*, NFCA, 1991.

Unequal Opportunities: Children with disabilities and their families speak out, NCH, 1994.

Fostering Children with Disabilities: A guide for carers, NFCA, 1991.

Oswin M, *Am I Allowed to Cry? A study of bereavement amongst people who have learning difficulties*, Souvenir Press, 1993.

Robinson C, *Home and Away: Respite care in the community*, Venture Press, 1991.

Russell P, *Short-term Care: A parent's perspective*, NCB, 1994.

Russell P, *The Children Act 1989 and Disability*, NCB, 1992.

Russell P, 'A challenge for child protection procedures' in Owen H and Pritchard J (eds), *Good Practice in Child Protection: A manual for professionals*, Jessica Kingsley, 1993.

Weshcott H and Cross M, *This Far and no Further – Towards ending the sexual abuse of children and adolescents*, BASW, 1996.

Wolkind S (ed), *Medical Aspects of Adoption and Foster Care*, Heinemann, 1979.

Appendix E
Useful organisations

Adoption Service
Thomas Coram Foundation, 40 Brunswick Square
London WC1N 1AZ

Advisory Centre for Education
22-24 Highbury Grove, London N5 2EA

Association for all Speech Impaired Children and Young People
347 Central Markets, Smithfield, London EC1A 9NH

BAAF*Link*
MEA House, Ellison Place
Newcastle-upon-Tyne NE1 8XS
(nationwide linking service for children needing new families)

Be My Parent
Skyline House, 200 Union Street, London SE1 0LX
(family finding service)

Barnardo's Family Placement Projects
(8 regional schemes) Head Office, Tanners Lane
Barkingside, Essex 1G6 1QS

Children in Scotland
Princes House, 5 Shandwick Place
Edinburgh EH2 4RG
(agency for organisations and individuals working with children and their families in Scotland)

Contact a Family
16 Sutton Ground, London SW1P 2PH
(information on support groups)

Council for Disabled Children
National Children's Bureau, 8 Wakley Street
London EC1V 7QE

Disability Alliance
Universal House, 88-94 Wentworth Street
London E1 7SA
(information on welfare rights)

Disabled Living Foundation
380-384 Harrow Road
London W9 2HU
(information on aids and adaptations)

Down's Syndrome Association
153-155 Mitcham Road, London SW7 9PG

ENABLE
6th Floor, 7 Buchanan Street, Glasgow G1 3HL
(for people with learning difficulties and their families in Scotland)

In Touch
10 Norman Road, Sale, Cheshire M33 3DE
(puts families who have children with similar disabilities in touch with each other)

Independent Adoption Service
121 Camberwell Road, London SE5 0HB

Mencap
(list of local branches available on request)
123 Golden Gate, London EC1Y 0RT

Parents for Children
41 Southgate Road, London N1 3JP
(specialist family finders)

PPIAS
Lower Boddington, Daventry
Northants NN11 6BY
(photo listing service for children with special needs)

Scope (for people with cerebral palsy)
12 Park Crescent, London W1N 4EQ
National free Helpline 0800 626 216

Sense (National Deaf and Blind Rubella Association)
11-13 Clifton Terrace
London N4 3SR

SPOD
286 Camden Road, London N1 0BH
(association for sexual and personal relationships of disabled people)

Tavistock Clinic
120 Belsize Lane, London NW3 5BA
(Valerie Sinason, psychiatrist, specialises in working with children and young people with disabilities)